"This story is a realistic survivor series. The winner's prize wasn't one million dollars and television recognition; it was and is peace of mind and freedom. The author uses drama and humor to guide us through her process of dealing with (and healing) her deep wounds —and rising from the ashes. She is a great role model for those of you who have been beaten down by family and/or life."

—Dr. Richard L. Travis, *Psychotherapist*

"A powerful story that touched my heart deeply. Her incredible journey, of transforming some extremely daunting circumstances into triumphs, made me laugh and even shed a few tears. She's a living testimony to the strength and courage of the human spirit. "

—Dr. Gregory Antyuhin, *Medical Intuitive*

"Riveting, inspiring, and eloquently written to say the least . . . Simon's resilience and determination, to not only survive but also beat the odds, is remarkable."

—Elaine Roberts, founder of
ER Body and Spirit Care

Against the Tide

Against the Tide

A True Story of Survival

Shoshanah Simon

Authors Choice Press
New York Lincoln Shanghai

Against the Tide
A True Story of Survival

Authors Choice Press
an imprint of iUniverse, Inc.

For information address:
iUniverse, Inc.
2021 Pine Lake Road, Suite 100
Lincoln, NE 68512
www.iuniverse.com

Originally published by Peaches n' Pearls Publishing

Cover design by: Angel Penland, Image Graphics 2000
Cover painting in part: Herbert James Draper, *Flying Fish*, 1910. Courtesy of Peter Nahum at the Leicester Galleries, London, England.

ISBN: 0-595-30166-5

Printed in the United States of America

This book is dedicated to Sandra Folsom and Lela Duckwitz. Their absence sent me searching for the pearl within.

This book is also dedicated to Gertrude Kussner and Opal Gibson. Their presence taught me how to culture the pearl once I discovered it.

Author's Notes

This is a work of nonfiction. In an effort to protect the privacy of others, I have changed their names and some of their physical features.

Life shrinks or expands in proportion to one's courage.

Anaïs Nin

Yes, you are a marvel. And when you grow up, can you then harm another who is, like you, a marvel? You must work—we all must work—to make the world worthy of its children.

Pablo Casals

1

While sunbeams danced through the windows of my parent's bedroom and onto the bureau mirror, another spring morning greeted me with a shimmering stance. I was an infant resting in my mother's arms as she breast-fed me. My sister Julia, who was six years old, was standing behind us and brushing the cape of sienna curls that caressed Mom's shoulders. She set the brush down on top of the mahogany bureau and attempted to measure the length of her own hair. She pulled some of her tawny tresses down around her face and asked, "Mommy, when is my hair going to be long like yours?"

Mom looked up and into Julia's hazel eyes that were reflected in the mirror. "Soon enough," she answered. Then her blue eyes looked down to return my gaze.

As my hand became like a paintbrush and she the canvas, a mural to depict the special bond between us began. I outlined her satin shoulders and graceful neck with long strokes, and I shaded her porcelain cheeks with tiny grasps. Then I sketched her narrow chin and dainty nose with delicate and featherlike touches. When I painted her tender smile, my precious portrait was complete. She drew me near, and her lips that were laced in rose met my forehead. She kissed and nibbled her way around my face and hands.

When I was finished nursing, she carried me over to the rocking chair that was in a corner of the room and next to the four poster bed. While Mom and I swayed back and forth, Julia sat on the edge of the bed and waited for me to let out a belch. Once I did, she asked, "Can I hold Peaches?"

"Maybe when she wakes up from her nap. If you sing to her, she'll fall asleep faster." When Julia began to sing a nursery rhyme, Mom winced and rubbed her head.

"Do you have a headache again?"

"It must be another migraine because my head feels like it's going to explode." Mom had a history of high blood pressure and suffered from migraines often.

"Do you want me to get your pills?"

"Okay, sweetie. I think I left them on the kitchen counter next to the stove. And please bring me a glass of water and some crackers. I'm getting sick to my stomach."

Julia dashed out of the room and down the hall. My sister, Rachel, who was nine years old; Jay, who was eight years old; and Joshua, who was four years old, were in the living room watching television. This distracted Julia, so she joined them. Meanwhile, I fell asleep to the irregular beat of Mom's troubled heart, and she laid me to rest in the bassinet. When my siblings heard Mom scream for help several minutes later, they rushed into the bedroom. She had been in the master bathroom vomiting and had staggered over to the bed. Julia and Rachel rushed over to her with a look of terror on their faces, and Jay and Joshua stood in the doorway in a state of bewilderment. "Call Daddy . . . something bad is happening to me," Mom said in between moans.

They reached Father at work, and he called his mother, Opal (Nana), who lived nearby. When Nana arrived, Mom was incoherent. Nana contacted Mom's cardiologist right away. By the time the doctor arrived, however, Mom was already slipping into a coma. Due to a cerebral hemorrhage, she had suffered a stroke. As the paramedics strapped her to the stretcher and placed her inside the ambulance, Julia hit one of them with her fists repeatedly and cried out, "Don't take our mommy away!" Rachel, Jay, and Joshua latched onto Nana, unwilling to let her go. While the ambulance disappeared from view, its siren echoed her farewell lullaby.

My siblings and I took shelter in Nana's warm embrace, and she took turns holding and rocking us throughout the next few nights. All the while, Mom's shadow followed us into the storm, and the scent of her lingered throughout the house. Our teardrops fell into torrential downpours until dazzling prisms of sunlight peaked through the mourning pains. Her luminous silhouette faded with the rain, and her spirit went into the *light*. She passed away exactly three weeks after her twenty-seventh birthday. I attempted to follow her, but I didn't make it beyond the valley. And that's when my climb up a mountain of adversity began.

2

So there was Father, left to raise four children and an infant without a wife. Nana and Pop virtually moved in to help him. The grief and strain took their toll, especially on Pop, since Mom had become like the daughter he never had. Sadly, five weeks later Pop had a heart attack, and the angel of death showed up on our doorstep once more. Shortly after Mom's unexpected and sudden departure, the blood running through Father's veins had already begun to chill. Thus, the second shock of losing his father merely solidified the sheets of isolation that were covering his heart.

Mom and Pop's memorial services were held at the same funeral parlor. Father didn't take home Mom's ashes after her service, and he told the funeral director to dispose of them. The director retained the ashes, assuming that when Father was no longer distraught, he would be back to get them. But then when Pop died not long after and they still hadn't heard from Father, they gave Mom's ashes to Nana. She took the ashes of Nicholas and Casandra Riann and had them buried next to each other in the family cemetery on Riann Avenue in Hopkinsville, Kentucky. Nana's act of kindness and respect was kept a secret from Father for awhile. When he finally did discover what she had done, it was the beginning of a major rift between the two of them. The dragon emerged thereafter, and we discovered the dark side of our daddy.

By July, when we were visiting relatives during our summer vacation, Father was already busy planning his future with another woman, Helen, sending her love letters from Michigan. Helen was no stranger. Besides being our previous baby sitter, she was also a member of the congregation of Jehovah's Witnesses, where Father served as the presiding elder. Though Nana was opposed to the idea, he married Helen on what would've been his and Mom's eleventh wedding anniversary. No one blamed him for wanting to find us a permanent caretaker as soon as possible. Or at least that was the rationale he used to satisfy his desires to be sexually intimate again. In other words, as a Witness, if he had sex and wasn't married, it was grounds for him to lose his position as an elder. And he would seriously run the risk of being excommunicated. He was a good provider. He didn't abuse alcohol or drugs, and he didn't gamble. Nevertheless, because he wed a nineteen-year-old within five months of losing his first wife, his ability to use discernment came into question.

Suspicion stirred as to whether the selfish side of his manhood had tempted him to stray. What raised doubtful eyebrows even higher, though, was that we weren't allowed to display any pictures of Mom or mention her name. Doing so caused us grief, and we were caught in between Father and Helen's crossfire. Helen displayed her distemper by slamming doors or giving Father the cold shoulder. Questions arose as to why she was so threatened over a dead woman. When he dismissed the idea that the covetous weeds had taken root while Mom was alive and Helen's jealousy toward her had lingered, these were quieted. Instead, he praised the outstanding courage that Helen showed by taking on a man with five children. And as a result, she was awarded the immediate respect and title as "Mother" or "Mom." Failing to address her appropriately resulted in some kind of punishment—usually a spanking.

Prior to Helen's rule, spankings usually entailed being swatted a few times on the backside. We were introduced to Father's belt only if we behaved badly. Since her reign, though, we became better acquainted with the tail of the dragon. In fact, we met the entire collection. There were wide tails, skinny tails, leather tails, and vinyl tails. Helen's favorite was the bare tail. Father never questioned if it was right or wrong—it just was.

Even though the childhood fairy tales Father had been told had duped him, he was determined to fulfill the fantasy to walk on water. In his attempt to follow in Jesus' footsteps, he set out to father twelve children. Helen was happy to oblige by giving birth to their first child, Jack, right before my second birthday. Kara was born two years later, and Beth was born the year after. Before long, we grew out of the house we were living in, so we moved to a larger one in the neighborhood.

After Nana's early attempt to undermine Helen's maternal nature and expose her shortcomings to Father failed, she was not allowed to see us without their supervision. We often found her hiding out in her Cadillac somewhere near our school. As we started to walk home, she would find us. Then once we were safely inside her car, she would take us to an ice cream parlor or convenience store for a treat. Thereafter, she would drop us off at the end of our street, where we promised to keep our rendezvous a secret. An impromptu meeting that she had with the vice-principal of my school, Mrs. Dees, one afternoon when I was in first grade, is what pushed her over the edge enough to intervene again.

The school day had ended, and Joshua and I were leaving the grounds when I saw Nana standing at the front loading zone. I ran to greet her. She held out her arms and shouted, "Peaches! How's my baby doing today?"

As she leaned down to kiss me on the cheek, I inhaled her sweet fragrance. "Nana, you smell good!"

"I'm so hungry I could eat a peach." She nibbled playfully on my shoulder. "You don't mind if I take a little bite, do you?"

After I giggled, I said, "I save all my peaches just for you."

"That's my girl. You know I can't make my favorite pie in the whole world if you're sharing them with everyone else." A bolt of lightning illuminated a gray blanket of clouds that were closing in on us. Joshua was straggling behind and looking over his shoulder periodically. "Hurry, Josh!" Nana said. "It's going to pour."

The scream of thunder startled him, and he collided with Mrs. Dees. "Pay attention, Josh, and watch where you're going," Mrs. Dees said. She placed an arm around his shoulder and escorted him to the car. Nana was holding the car door open, and I was sitting on the front seat. Joshua got in and sat on the backseat. Mrs. Dees asked Nana, "Are you Josh's grandmother?"

"Yes."

"Can I have a few minutes of your time?" Mrs. Dees asked.

"Okay. Is something wrong?"

"It's better if we go back inside to my office . . . where it's private."

Nana said to Joshua and I, "Stay in the car. I'll

be back soon."

When they were out of sight, Joshua said, "I hope Mrs. Dees doesn't tell on me."

"For what?" I asked.

"I know that she saw me saluting the flag when she came into my class this morning."

I put my hands up to my mouth. "Um! You're going to get destroyed at Armageddon with all the wicked people." Then I shoved a few jellybeans into my mouth.

He leaned forward and opened my lunch bag and noticed that it was full of forbidden-fruited candy and other goodies. "I guess you will, too. But first Mother's going to whip you when she finds out that you've been eating Easter candy." He noticed that I was becoming slightly anxious. He smiled and took out a wrapped chocolate bunny and shoved it into his lunch bag. "Well, I guess this could be our secret."

"I won't tell if you won't." I counted the remaining pieces of candy that were in my bag before I asked, "How come you salute the flag?"

"There are these three punks in my class. They're threatening to beat me up if they catch me not saluting the flag again. Now half the class is calling me a *commie*."

"What's a *commie*?"

"Beats me . . . Johnny Pinko said his father didn't get half his leg blown off in Vietnam for people like us who don't vote and fight for our freedom."

"Ew yuk! He doesn't have a leg?"

"Nope."

"Did you tell Daddy they want to beat you up?"

"Yes. But he told me to give them the *Watchtower* and invite them to a Sunday meeting. I swear I get so sick of going to the meetings three times a week."

8

"Me, too," I said. "All the good shows are always on a meeting night." Once I finished chewing another mouthful of jellybeans, I asked, "What's that smell?"

"I don't smell anything . . . maybe it's your breath."

"You're the one who never brushes your teeth," I said.

After we were done teasing each other, we resorted to playing tic-tac-toe until Nana came back to the car.

We attended meetings at the kingdom hall three times a week; two hours on Sunday mornings and Thursday evenings; and one hour on Tuesday evenings. If we didn't verbally participate in the question-and-answer period at the meetings, we feared getting a spanking or losing a privilege. In addition to preparing for those meetings, my brothers had to give an oral report on an article out of the latest *Watchtower* magazine on Tuesdays and Thursdays during dinner. Likewise, on Mondays and Wednesdays my sisters and I had to give an oral report on an article out of the *Awake* magazine. Finally, while other children were at home Saturday mornings catching up on their sleep or watching cartoons, we were like little soldiers, getting doors closed on us as we spread the "good news."

Witnesses attract outsiders with their message of the wicked being cleansed from the earth during Armageddon, and faithful servants who dedicate their lives to preaching their gospel will be rewarded with eternal life on a paradise earth. After a kind and friendly reception, followers are encouraged to give up their worldly pursuits, for the end of the world is always just around the corner. All the while, a whole life span has passed and they have nothing more than regrets to show for the relationships and unrequited hopes and dreams that they've sacrificed. Regrettably, anyone in their life who doesn't accept their message or tries to encourage them to exercise independent thinking is cut off from further association. Any friend or family member who isn't interested in converting is either cut off entirely or kept at a distance. Though many aren't familiar with their ideologies and regard them as a harmless religious organization, their isolation and alienation tactics put them into the cult category. An example of this fanaticism and control is that they discourage getting a college education. Even if they're athletically inclined or their abilities could earn them a scholarship, Witnesses are prohibited from engaging in sports unless it's an academic requirement. So although I often wanted to join the swim or track team, it was out of the question. Holding office in any school clubs or outside organizations is also forbidden. And perhaps the well-known restriction, which sets them apart from most of the other organized religions, is that they're not allowed to celebrate birthdays or national holidays. Some Witnesses rigidly adhere to these doctrines; some draw the lines when it comes to family; and some make up their own rules as they go along.

"Bad association spoils useful habits." This was a scripture that was quoted in my house from *their* Bible like a chant. Any contact with the world outside was basically forbidden, and it was very difficult keeping friends in school. If I was invited to spend the night with classmates or go to a birthday party, it always ended embarrassingly because I had to refuse the invitation. As a result, I felt like I never fit in.

When Nana returned to the car, she barely spoke two words on the drive over to the ice cream parlor. When I finished eating my banana split, she persuaded me to entertain myself and gave me several quarters so that I could play pinball. She and Joshua stayed inside the booth, talking. I don't know what they discussed. I only noticed that he lost his appetite, and Nana was getting madder by the moment. But her anger wasn't directed at him.

By the time we headed home and were approaching the end of our street, the worst of the thunderstorm had passed. When Nana saw Helen's van parked in the driveway, she said, "Don't get out yet. I'm coming home with you. I want to talk to Helen." Joshua and I looked at each other. "Don't worry. Someone had to make sure that you didn't walk home in this storm—since *Queen* Helen could care less."

When Nana walked inside the house, two laundry baskets full of clean linens were sitting on the floor in the family room. Jay was on the couch doing home-work. She kissed him on the cheek and then went into the kitchen, where Rachel was browning meat in a pot on the stove. Julia was filling baby bottles at the bar in the kitchen. After she kissed them both, she took the receiver off the telephone that was hanging on the wall and listened for a dial tone. "Is Helen taking a nap?" Nana asked. "The line's been busy all afternoon."

"Yes," Rachel answered. "She probably took the phone off the hook."

"I need to speak to her," Nana said.

"She told us not to bother her when she's taking a nap," Julia said.

"That's too bad," Nana said sarcastically. "Looks like I'll just have to wake up sleeping beauty." She walked through the kitchen and into the nursery. Father and Helen's bedroom was directly off the nursery. After Nana knocked on the door twice, Helen opened it and Nana went inside.

11

Nana came out of the room about ten minutes later and Helen yelled, "Joshua, get your butt in here now!"

"Don't punish him, Helen," Nana said. "It was probably an accident."

"I don't care what his excuse is," Helen responded. "He's too old to be crapping in his pants! We didn't tolerate it from Jay, and we're certainly not going to tolerate it from him."

When Joshua came out of the bedroom moments later, he was whimpering. He went into the family room, sat on the floor, and began folding laundry with Nana and I. "Did she spank you?" Nana asked softly.

Helen walked into the kitchen with a foul look. "I'm leaving that for his father." She lifted the top off the pot and stirred the simmering beef. Then she slammed the metal spoon down on top of the stove. "Thank you, Opal, for bringing them home. Now go."

"I'm waiting for Harry to come home," Nana said.

"As soon as he gets home, we're eating dinner quickly because it's a meeting night," Helen said. "And he's giving the talk tonight, so he has to look over his notes."

"What I have to say won't take long," Nana said.

"Suit yourself." Helen replied, then she directed her attention toward Joshua and I. "When you two are done putting the clothes away, there's another load in the washer that needs to be hung out on the line. Then set the table for dinner." She walked through the nursery and turned around before she went into her bedroom and spoke to me. "Shoshanah, since you didn't do a satisfactory job cleaning the bathroom before you left for school this morning, you'll be clearing off the table after dinner—not Joshua." All the commotion awoke Kara, who was two years old, and Beth, who was one. Their cries sent Julia and Rachel into the nursery. When Helen heard Jack's cries moments later, she opened her bedroom door. "Did my little goober wake up from his nap?" He grinned widely and ran over to her. "Hurry," she stated, "before all the cool air disappears." When he crossed the threshold, she shut the door.

By five o'clock, Father was home. As soon as Nana saw him parking his truck in the driveway, she went outside to meet him. Helen was putting the stew and biscuits on the dining room table while Rachel was filling the glasses with ice. Jay, Julia, and I were in the front yard playing with Jack, Kara, and Beth. Father, exasperated and tired, listened to Nana briefly. Then he responded, shook his head, and walked away. When she continued to badger him, he shouted, "That's enough! You've had it in for Helen from the beginning. If you don't mind your own business and let us raise *our* children as we see fit, you won't see them again. I don't care how much they beg me."

"Casandra's children haven't known a happy day since you married that Jezebel," Nana said. "And I'm not going to stand by and watch the rest of their childhoods wasted on doing the things that she should be doing. I won't hesitate to fight to get custody of them if I have to. Someone has to protect them." She went inside only long enough to get her purse and say good-bye to Rachel and Joshua. When she came back outside, Father met her at the front door. She leaned down and whispered in my ear, "Don't worry, Nana's not going to leave you."

"Quit poisoning her mind and go home," Father said.

The next time we saw Nana was a few days later at the Memorial. (The Memorial holds the same significance to Witnesses as Easter does to Christians. It represents Jesus' death and resurrection.) We sat silently throughout the entire ceremony. We were forbidden from sampling a piece of heaven, the bread that represented Jesus' body. And stealing a sip of wine and indulging in the cup of freedom that symbolized his blood was also off limits to us. We weren't of the chosen few—the one hundred and forty-four thousand. According to their beliefs, these are the only mortals who are granted a pass into heaven. Our lowly merit allowed us only to reside in the servant's quarters, where our master anointed us with oils of guilt. As Father led the congregation to celebrate this event, it was another one of his golden moments to shine in glory.

Once the celebration ended, he drooled over the praise that the congregation sprinkled his ego with. With power and control being his drug of choice, his charisma intoxicated some into idolatry. When he flashed them his human side, they drew the shades and closed the shutters. The upstanding image in his organization was the delusive backdrop to preserve the perfect picture and deter outsiders from seeing what went on behind the scenes. However, as Nana stood in the background while family snapshots were taken, she was realizing how dangerous his addiction had become. She couldn't take the insidious invasion anymore. She was torn between seeing her grandchildren being neglected and abused versus being forbidden to see them at all. Thus, by the end of the school year she went into cardiac arrest.

Nana's treating Helen as though she wasn't fit to break bread with made Father's jowls salivate with an angry appetite for revenge. When Nana lay dying in the trenches, he couldn't resist striking her with another fatal blow. He denied Julia's request to say good-bye, telling her that hospital policy didn't allow her in the room because of her age. My siblings and I lost our greatest ally later that evening. She died of a *broken heart* while serving in combat. Nevertheless, being the matriarch that she always was, she fired the last round and had the last word by bequeathing her two homes to her oldest son and not to Father.

When I saw her lifeless body lying in the casket and touched her cold hand, I was old enough to comprehend that she wasn't coming home. Yet I was too young to comprehend that she was never going to hug, kiss, or sing to me again. I soon realized that it would be years before I ever felt cared for or heard the words of love uttered to me again. The dreadfulness of being abandoned snuck into the back door of my childhood dreams when I wasn't looking, and the spirited little girl known as "Peaches" vanished.

Like Nana, I tried to give Helen a chance. After all, she was the only mother I knew. She was nice and fun to be around as long as you followed orders and kept your mouth shut. But even when I did, I tried to figure out what was wrong with me and why at times she could be so cruel—like the time she took me home from the hospital following my tonsilectomy. Even though I could tolerate only smooth foods, I was thrilled that we were going to a restaurant for lunch and not directly home. I was content nibbling on my ice cream. Nonetheless, she ordered a cola for me and insisted that I drink it to soothe my fresh incision.

Living without Mom was hard. But being the last souvenir of her desertion and the sharpest thorn remaining in Helen's rose garden was even worse. Whenever Helen was out of earshot and relatives were visiting us, they often mentioned that my expressions and characteristics were eerily similar to Mom's. So being the one out of all her children who physically resembled her the most was to my misfortune. I was a constant reminder of her betrayal and a past that Father couldn't run from.

Having younger siblings made me happy most of the time, especially when Helen bore her last child, Kate. By the time she came along, I was ten. Everyone doted on her because she was the youngest and only child in our family who had blue eyes. I enjoyed dressing her for meetings, and her cries, which often sent me to the lobby of the kingdom hall, were a good excuse to get out of what I considered to be brainwashing sessions. Caring for her distracted me from the moments of malevolence that I had toward my other younger siblings. This wasn't because I wanted to be the center of the universe. Rather, it was because I craved the love and affection that I thought Helen and Father were giving to them and not to me. This aggravated me to the bottom of my belly, for I knew that there was no way that I could compete with them, though I tried.

As a teenager, Helen knew that I was saving for a car. So in exchange for doing the laundry on the weekends, she paid me five dollars a week. By then, we had two washers and two dryers to keep up with the demands of a large household. If the laundry wasn't done on a daily basis, by the time the weekend approached the two plastic trashcans that were used as hampers were overflowing. As Father was getting dressed for a meeting one night, he came to me and asked, "Why don't I have any clean dress shirts?" I didn't bother defending myself, explaining that Helen didn't do the laundry all week and was letting it pile up for me on the weekends. Instead, I changed my routine and did a few loads of laundry every day after school.

Finally, one night during dinner, when Father was complaining about the high grocery bill, I added, "If Kara, Beth, and Kate put their clothes into their dressers instead of throwing them on the floor when they go to bed at night, then I wouldn't have to do as much laundry. It would save some of the money that you spend on electric and laundry detergent."

"Why aren't you putting them in the drawers for them?" Father asked me. From then on I knew it was pointless. I didn't even bother asking why it was that whenever one of Helen's children got sick and couldn't do the dishes, I had to do them. But then, whenever I became ill and it was my night to do the dishes, the dishes sat there until the following night when I had to do all of them.

These trivial injustices and blatant acts of favoritism couldn't compare to the cold-hearted detachment that I experienced when I took a desperate measure to reach out to Father and Helen.

I was fourteen when I thought that ingesting twenty diet pills would spark the reaction I was dying for. It was early one Sunday morning when I decided to take the pills. I was in the midst of getting dressed when they took effect. Because I was focused only on getting the result I wanted, I wasn't prepared for the consequences, so I panicked. My heart felt like it was going to beat out of my chest. I sent Kara to ask Helen to come to my room.

When several minutes passed and Helen didn't come to see me, I went to her. When I knocked on their bedroom door, she came to the door but didn't open it. "What is it?" she asked.

"I don't know what to do. I'm scared. I don't know what made me do it, but I took a bunch of diet pills." I heard her say something to Father, but I couldn't make out what it was. When I heard him responding to her, I added, "I'm sorry. I didn't mean to do it."

"Try to vomit as much of the pills up as you can," Helen said. "Then I want you to get dressed. You're going to the meeting!"

I did what I was told. I managed to finish dressing with the exception of fixing my hair. In the meantime, my heart felt like an accelerator, speeding up and then slowing down to a crawl. While the rest of the family was getting in the van, I was still in my bedroom, laying on the bed. After Father blew the horn and I didn't come out, Helen went back into the house. She stood in the doorway of my bedroom and said, "Quit being a hypochondriac and get your butt in the van."

When I climbed into the van, I immediately went back and laid across the rear seat. My heart fluttered faster with every turn. Everything was spinning, sweat coated my clammy skin, and my limbs were numb with fear. Once Father drove into the parking lot of the kingdom hall, I waited for everyone else to get out of the van. He waited for me to come out, but I stayed on the seat. "I can't go in. I feel very sick. Please let me stay out here."

He took off his belt and threatened to hit me. However, being in the parking lot with spectators from the congregation walking by made it difficult for him to carry out his threat. So he left me there in the sweltering heat while he went inside. Ten minutes later, Ted, another elder and the father of a daughter whom I often baby-sat, came out to see me. "I noticed that you weren't inside, so I asked Kara where you were," he said. "I hope you don't mind." I continued to lay there silently. "You don't look so good. Are you okay?"

"I tried to tell them that I don't feel well, but they won't listen to me."

"What's wrong?"

"I know it was stupid. But I took a bunch of diet pills early this morning. I've already vomited up everything that was in my stomach. I feel dizzy, hot, and have the chills—all at the same time."

He touched my face. "It's going to be okay. Do you want me to take you to the emergency room?"

"Whatever you think."

"I'll be back in a few minutes," he said.

Ted went back inside, but my disgruntled father returned. He was unhappy that his parental authority was questioned and that he was forced to put on a caring facade. His position in the congregation made most Witnesses quake with fear at the mere thought of questioning his actions. Apparently, the opinions of his congregation held greater significance than his daughter's feelings.

Father didn't take me to the emergency room to make sure that I was out of physical danger. Instead, he took me home, where I laid on his and Helen's bed. As far as he was concerned, I was lucky to escape a session with the tail of the dragon and the tropical heat and to be recovering in the only air-conditioned bedroom in the house. But I knew this was for his benefit and not mine. He didn't want the sweat rolling down his cheeks while he was reading the Sunday newspaper.

His ears went deaf as he ignored my cries for attention. "Mommy, help me, please." He knew it was *my* mother I was crying for and not Helen because I never referred to Helen as anything but "Mother."

19

I wanted to shake him out of his oblivion.

*Come here my precious Peaches and sit on Daddy's lap.
What made you go to such lengths to capture my attention?
Tell me where it hurts. What can I do to make you know
that I do love you and your feelings do count? I never
meant to hurt my precious Peaches.*

Fantasy.

Father pulled the newspaper down a couple of
inches, just barely enough to look over at me. The only
condolence he offered was this: "You should have
known better than to be so stupid and take all those
diet pills. If you really want to kill yourself, you don't
do it with diet pills. It serves you right for getting sick.
Maybe this will teach you a lesson." Then he returned
to reading the comic section, laughing periodically at
the material that entertained him. His neglect branded
me with one of the most damaging messages a father
could ever send to his child: *Your feelings don't count
because you're nothing.* I had to realize that it didn't
matter what my needs or wants were because the only
feelings that counted were his. My hopes were
dashed, and I had to accept, *you were never Daddy's
little girl, nor will you ever be.*

I did learn a powerful lesson that day when Ted—
not Father or Helen—called me later that evening to
see how I was doing. Though Father and Helen were
having dinner with Ted and his wife, neither of them
got on the telephone to talk to me. My physical,
emotional, and mental condition didn't even enter
their thoughts. They were too wrapped up in themselves and having a good time. Their total disregard
that I was an individual and not just one of their
religious servants or house slaves made me feel like I
was already dead. I thought that experiencing the
physical pain, if I would've carried out my death wish,

would not have hurt half as much as the emotional agony I had to endure by staying alive. From that day forward, it was as if a corpse became my epitome and I was forced to live inside a morgue with parents who were already emotionally dead themselves. My trust started to wane, for it seemed like everyone who ever meant anything to me had let me down.

No one could have imagined what was truly behind my cry for help and the modus operandi I was forced to use to keep myself physically alive. Nor would they have fathomed that when the fourth of September passed each year—and Father and Helen had parties to celebrate their anniversary—a silent killer was rejoicing. The assassin was filled with a guilty pleasure in assuming that they had gotten away with murder. Hence, the day they wed was the last day of my childhood innocence; and from then on I was forced to grow up sooner than my years allowed.

While Father was busy building his delusional dynasty, I took refuge in a realm of fantasy. Writing in my diary became my sanctuary, where I kept my thoughts hidden under lock and key. I was too young to realize that my soul was searching for an antidote to cure my aching heart. I discovered a resource that temporarily patched the holes inside me. The Bible verse Father quoted many times from his pulpit, "The truth shall set you free," did anything but. The grim reality of what my childhood was turning into imprisoned my thoughts and shaded my soul black. My words liberated me, and I waited for my prince to come and rescue me.

3

Lauren stood, with a beer and cigarette in one hand and a remote control in the other, surfing through the channels of her television. Suddenly astonished, she paused and took a step back. "Hey, I know that guy. That's Evan, Daniel's roommate. And that's where I've been going lately to do my laundry." Evan Cauffman, a young entrepreneur who recently opened a dry cleaners and laundromat in one of the poorest areas of the county, was being interviewed by a journalist from a local television station.

"Is that the same Daniel that you want to introduce me to?" I asked.

Lauren grinned. "Mm-hm."

I got up off the leather couch and took the remote control from her and turned up the volume. Evan stood proudly in front of his new business, exuding just enough arrogance without being obnoxious. I admired his ambition and allowed his tenacious tale of American capitalism at its best to captivate me. When the brief interview was over, I remarked, "Well forget about Daniel. I want to meet the next Donald Trump."

Lauren laughed, tilted her head of dark-blonde hair backward, and rolled her china-blue eyes. Then she took a sip of beer and a drag from the cigarette. At twenty-five, the wrinkles surrounding her mouth, due to her habit of inhaling since she was an early teen, physically matured her a decade beyond her youth. "So you prefer the brainy type?"

"Always," I said. "And the sports car doesn't hurt either."

"Funny . . ."

"What?"

"I just thought that you and Daniel would make a cute couple. He's got the surfer look—you know blonde hair and blue eyes. Hell, if I wasn't married, I wouldn't mind riding a few waves with him. "

"Looks aren't everything," I said. My curious appetite was becoming wet with wonder. "So . . . does Evan have a girlfriend?"

"I don't know, but I'm sure I can find out. Hey, why don't you come with me the next time I go do laundry? He usually pops in and out. Maybe he'll be there."

I strutted across the living room. "Sounds like a plan. In the meantime, let me see what lingerie I can roundup that will need his expertise."

She laughed, then said, "You go girl!"

I rented the garage apartment behind the Spanish, Mediterranean style house where Lauren and her husband lived with their two daughters. The streets in the neighborhood were paved with winos who made the alleyways their homes. Prostitutes also used the alleys to turn tricks in the backseats of cars, and barefoot children with runny noses paraded the sidewalks. Though everything screamed poverty to me and the depressing setting fueled my ambition and motivation to succeed, it was a dangerous place to live. Home invasions and car thefts were commonplace. So because Lauren's husband's job often took him out of town and I was a young woman living alone, we looked out for each other. Her daughters seemed to enjoy my company as much I did theirs—getting on their level came natural to me. This, and the close proximity, bonded our friendship.

During the rinse cycle, my satin panties, lace bras, and I made an alluring introduction. As Wham! blared from the speakers that hung in each corner of the laundromat, I held Megan, Lauren's four-year-old, and swung her around in circles while Lauren and Daniel danced. Then I grabbed my hairbrush from my purse, pretended it was a microphone, and slaughtered some of the lyrics. Megan giggled and Lauren yelled in between her own laughter, "You're a nut!"

I paused from my poor rendition to respond, "I'm always the last to know."

"Doesn't Daniel resemble George Michael?" Lauren asked.

"Indulge in your fantasies," I said. Daniel glared at me disapprovingly. "I take that back. Georgie boy couldn't hold a candle to you."

He winked at me and replied, "It looks like she won't be needing glasses after all."

Evan roused even more amusement when he came up behind us clapping. He joined in, "Don't be so sure Don Juan. I have a great optometrist who I can recommend her to." I cast him a playful grin. He extended his hand. "Welcome to my washbowl. I'm Evan. Do you have any other talents besides singing? I'm sorry, I didn't catch your name."

I put Megan down and gently grasped his hand. "Shoshanah . . . nice to meet you. I've never met someone who's been on television before."

"Oh, so you caught my acting debut."

"Most of it."

"Mr. Joe College makes it big when he snatches up an abandoned building on skid row," he said. I put the brush up to his mouth, and he entertained us further. "It's no longer a hooker hangout and shelter for crack heads. Joe's part of the clean sweep team in Palmwood. He plans on turning this place into a thriving hot spot where singles can mingle, play pool, have a brew or two, and get their clothes cleaned in the process."

Daniel walked over and grabbed the brush out of my hand and said, "Hey Joe, aren't you forgetting about your buddy?—the one who came up with the brilliant idea."

"Of course, without further ado, may I introduce one of the biggest womanizers in all of South Florida, Daniel LaVaugh? What a way to bring in the ladies. Oh dear," Evan pointed his index finger onto his cheek and continued, "I just can't get a handle on this laundry thing. The colors run into the whites, and the whites turn dull. I'm just a Daniel in distress. Now you don't have to go carousing the beach to find the babes. They can come to you."

Daniel walked away with his hands cupped over his face, pretending to be mortified. "My secret's out."

As they laughed, I took back the brush. "This is Shoshanah Riann reporting for *City Scenes*."

"You're a natural reporter," Evan said.

"You think so?"

"Is journalism your major?"

The final spin cycle on one of the washers that I was using had just finished, sparing me from having to disclose what I did for a living. "Excuse me." I began to take my clothes out of the washer and put them in the adjacent dryer.

"Let me help you." He began taking my clothes out of the other washer. When he noticed my choice in undergarment attire, he smiled. "I like your taste in fashion."

25

I flushed with excitement, hoping he didn't mistake my premeditated plan to arouse his interest for being promiscuous. "I'm glad you approve."

He finished helping me, then said, "I have to get back to work. It was nice meeting you. I hope to see more of you . . . and your wardrobe."

Within a month, Evan and I were casually dating. He seemed to be at ease in my company most of the time, relieved that I wasn't like the girls he grew up with. I was a simple woman who hadn't been spoiled and pampered. I didn't have high expectations, so I didn't have high standards that he had to measure up to. Because I was financially responsible for myself, I regarded anything as trivial as his buying me dinner and a drink like it was a royal treat.

We didn't see each other or talk on the telephone every day. Thus, I had a difficult time discerning whether what we shared was just a fleeting fling or something more. One of my concerns was that maybe he was using me as an instrument to evoke jealousy in Daniel. Although he disapproved of Daniel's indiscreet encounters with the opposite sex, he was envious of his ability to attract so many beautiful women. In his eyes, Daniel had all the preliminaries to win a woman over and get her into bed. He had sun-bleached hair, baby blues, an athlete's physique, and he spoke fluent French. At one point Evan even accused him of running an escort service. The villa that they shared on the other side of town, where the pretentious yuppies thrived, had a revolving door; one woman would no sooner be leaving and another woman was coming in. Despite the fact that Evan was short, had a receding hairline, and wore glasses, he was well educated and financially stable. Therefore, he couldn't understand why his own bed had been empty for so long. However, Daniel, who lacked education and money, always had soiled sheets and a pretty head resting on his pillows. If he won the affections of me—I thought—it would be one way for him to prove to himself that he was just as desirable as Daniel was. The plot thickened and my curiosity about his intentions intensified, especially after the night when he filled me with the hope that we could have something more permanent.

It was New Year's Eve and also my birthday, so Evan invited me out to celebrate both occasions. The restaurant where we went for dinner was on the intra-coastal waterway, and a scarlet-red lighthouse towered in the background. A whirlpool of currents echoed as they splashed against the wooden pier that draped the landscape. Among the cool mist rising, a tempered glow of crimson and gold lights, which trimmed the deck in holiday ornamentation, illuminated the water's surface, casting iridescent shadows upon it. Pelicans stood watch atop of the timber posts, mesmerized by the patrons docking their yachts.

We sat in a cozy corner out on the veranda. We had finished dinner and were sipping Tia Maria and coffee. "It looks like we might have to sell the business," Evan said.

"How come?"

"It's not bringing in the kind of revenue that we hoped it would."

"What about your plans to turn it into a pub?"

"I guess they're history. My parents are reluctant to put up any more money because of its location."

"What are you going to do if you sell it?—go back to being a stockbroker."

"I'm not so sure that's possible." He hesitated for a

moment. "The company that sponsored me said that they were going to blackball me from the industry."

"Why?"

"It's a long story. The contract that I signed with them was like my death certificate when I left. They're trying to sue me for the time that they invested in me."

"I'm sorry to hear that," I said.

"I haven't decided what I'm going to do yet. My family wants me to go to law school and become an attorney. Even though I'm dreading the thought of it, I'll probably end up going anyway."

"Even if your heart isn't in it?"

"I'm afraid so," he said. "I've already disappointed my parents enough. And since they put up the money for the business, I feel like I owe it to them to go."

When he shook his head, I could see the anguish in his face and hear the hint of despair in his words. "I'm sure they just want what's best for you," I said.

His fingers outlined the tips of my fingernails. "For me, or for them?" I didn't know what to say, so he continued, "I only wish everyone else didn't own me. Anyway, let's get off this heavy subject . . . and let's get back to celebrating." He smiled, leaned across the table, and said softly, "I hope you like the present I got you."

"What'd you get me?" I pleaded like an inquisitive child.

He shook his head. "No. You're going to have to be a good little girl and wait until we get back to my place." He stood up and briefly rested his chin on top of my head before I rose to his gesture. "Shall we go?"

When I met his gaze, my dark eyes burned with coal desire. "Patience isn't one of my stronger virtues. I'd hate to think of what I might do if I had to wait much longer."

His whisper tickled my ear. "For what? . . . your present or me."

"I thought you were my present."

He tore off the plastic covering and placed the new cassette in his car stereo. "Lauren told me that you didn't buy this cassette yet. This was playing the first day we met—remember?"

"I do."

He slid open the sunroof, which welcomed the seaside breezes and cooled our fevers that were burning for each other's touch. Then he pulled me close. "I hope you like it."

"Let me show you how much." My heart leaped with the dance of his bedroom eyes. My body shuddered when I welcomed the dark curls upon his well-defined chest, the remnants of which were poking out of his shirt, anxiously awaiting my strokes of admiration. I drowned in desire and plunged deeper into the scent of his cologne.

As he released the hair clips that were holding the beret in place that I was wearing, he returned my kisses softly and his lips lightly brushed against my neck. When my curls made their descent like a cascading waterfall, he whispered, "I've always loved your hair." We necked for several minutes.

When we went back to his villa, we nestled in each other's arms on the suede sectional and watched the celebration being broadcast from Times Square. His embrace enfolded me in a warm shelter of naked emotions. All the while, outside the winter winds waltzed in between the trees and the cedar shingles covering the rooftops shivered, as the midnight ghosts wrestled in the foreboding storm. We retired early, unable to arrest our ravenous urges to ring in the New Year of 1986 with loving sighs of replete.

As he carried me up the staircase, burnished moonlight penetrated the skylight above the landing and guided his steps. We fell lightly onto the silk sheets and celebrated our tender bodies union until our souls briefly converged to greet the dawn. We said little, allowing the mortal rhythm to resound the magical cadence in our love song. We slept peacefully for a few hours and awoke with rejuvenation. While showering, he tamed the curls on my head, dousing it with lather and gently massaging my scalp. Then his firm tongue molded each curve of my body with intricate detail, sculpturing me with wet kisses. I devoured him in his entirety.

I stood in front of the mirrored closet doors and combed my hair while he dressed. I was wearing his bathrobe that had his initials embossed just below the collar. "I like the way you look in my robe. Maybe one day I'll get you one to match."

"Will you get my initials sewn on it, too?"

"Even better. How about the initials SC?"

Our minds were traveling down different roads. "My last name doesn't begin with a C."

"I know . . . but mine does."

I responded to his charismatic expression with complete surprise. "Are you talking about marriage?"

"Not anytime soon. We'd have to wait a few years."

Though he caught me completely off guard, I played along. "Why's that?"

"My parents would probably accept you, but my grandparents wouldn't."

"Why not?"

"They're Orthodox Jews. They want me to marry in my faith. If I go against their wishes, they'll cut me out of their will. So I'll just have to wait until they're gone."

I didn't know what to say, other than, "I see." Minutes later, when I heard him play "Keeping the Faith" by Billy Joel on his stereo for the third time, I asked, "Why do you keep playing that song?"

He pulled me close. "I don't know. I guess because it makes me feel good."

"So what are your plans for today?"

"My family always gets together at my parent's house. I'd invite you, but I'm sure you don't want to sit around all afternoon watching football games."

"I think Lauren's having a party anyway. I'll probably hang out there."

Evan was the first man to ever bring up marriage. I hadn't had enough experience with men to differentiate whether he was using me for sexual pleasures or whether he sincerely cared about me. Though I kept my feelings to myself, I was hurt. I figured that he was ashamed of what I did for a living; that I was just a cleaning girl who lacked a college education. For my own self-preservation, I focused more on that possibility than on the real issue; that we came from different religious and socioeconomic backgrounds. Since a difference in religious beliefs is what wedged the estrangement between Father and I, those old familiar feelings of rejection encapsulated me. And now I was getting the same rejection from someone I was falling for and could envision a future with. I left with his flannel overcoat, trying to warm my world from the chilly reception that he was trying to shield me from should I dare enter his world. That morning his spirit went one way and mine went another.

I went out with him a couple of times after that. But when he continued to keep me away from his family, I stopped seeing him out of angry compulsion. Within weeks, Lauren informed me that he had started dating a Jewish girl whom his parents had set him up with. Shortly after this discovery, my spite drove me to resume my relationship with Jim, a man whom I had been on and off with for two years before Evan and I began to date. I knew that the news that I was living with someone would filter back to Evan somehow. I had mixed feelings about this. I was hoping to abet a response and make him realize that I wasn't sitting around brooding over him. Yet I didn't want him to see how low I could sink by making such a lousy choice. And I never expected to have their paths cross. Fate, however, intervened when I wished it hadn't.

I had been going to a different laundromat across town to avoid Evan altogether. But unbeknownst to me, Jim had dropped off some of his clothes to be dry-cleaned at his laundromat. When Jim called me from work and asked me to pick up the clothes, I looked for every excuse not to go. But he reminded me that it was Saturday and that the dry-cleaning section of the laundromat was closed on Sundays. So if he wanted to have clothes to wear to work on Monday, I had the choice of either swallowing my unease and running into Evan or getting into a fight with Jim.

When I went to the laundromat, Evan and his new girlfriend were sitting behind the counter. We exchanged introductions. Then I handed him the receipt for the laundry. As he was handing me the clothes, he asked, "Is the guy who dropped these off your boyfriend?"

I was busted. "Yes," I responded in enormous embarrassment.

He shook his head. "I can't believe it." My ignorance eluded me from the huge blow that this might have been to Evan's ego. The choice that I had made was to be with someone who did not hold a steady job;

32

whose face looked as though the Nazis had used it for target practice; and whose protruding stomach and flabby tone indicated a severe lack in physical fitness. Jim could've been a poster pinup for the American Cancer Society, showing teenagers what can happen if they get the nicotine monkey on their back and become a chain smoker like him. In contrast, although Evan would never be gracing the cover of any romance novels, he had warm and pleasing features. He also did weight training faithfully to keep his muscles flexed and his stomach behind his belt. I was ashamed that my low self-esteem bred me disrespect in one of the ugliest forms. And I was mortified that Evan was there to witness the disgraceful testimony.

Seeing Evan with his new girlfriend only made me more incensed. So shortly after, I turned around and did what I thought he had done to me. I certainly had no serious intentions of marrying Jim—especially since he had a vasectomy years earlier, and I knew that I wanted to have children one day. Nevertheless, I was going to use Jim anyway by manipulating him into proposing marriage to me.

After a few weeks, I finally got up the courage to return to Evan's laundromat since it was the closest one nearby. I waited until the early evening to go and do my laundry—not expecting him to be there. But fate intervened again, for as I was putting my clothes in my car, Evan stopped by. We made small talk for a few minutes. He congratulated me on my engagement, and I congratulated him on his acceptance into Nova in Miami.

His parents had decided to put the business up for sale. He was going to stay in the area to help his parents until the school term started. Then he planned to move to Miami and live with his grandparents while he went to school.

As we parted, he hugged me with great intensity—like I was a life preserver he had found among the rocky seas and he was hanging on to it for dear life. I dismissed my intuition. Instead, I let the anger of a painful childhood pattern repeating itself anchor my thoughts in obscurity. He pulled away, looked into my eyes and said, "I'm going to miss you."

4

When I met Jim, I was a clerk for the real estate office that was on the premises of Century Village, a predominantly Jewish residential community. Some of my duties included showing and inspecting condominiums that were for rental or resale and being the liaison between the landlords and their tenants. Jim was a maintenance man for the appliance service company that held the majority of service contracts in Century Village. So whenever any of the major appliances in the vacant condominiums were in need of repair or replacing, I usually called him.

Unlike Rachel and Julia, who got to experience seeing Father at his best during their formative years, by the time I arrived he was already falling from grace. When my prince didn't come calling for me by the time I was eighteen, I had to go looking for him. I was so desperate for any male's attention that even toads were tempting. In my flattery that someone of the male persuasion was giving me attention, I overlooked Jim's detrimental characteristics. I was too young and immature to realize that he was taking over where my childhood abusers left off. Like Helen, he was a lazy sponge; and like Father, he was very controlling.

His parents divorced when he was a teenager, and the picture that he painted was that he was the black sheep of his family. I felt compassion and empathy for him because he was treated as an outcast and left all alone in the big bad world. He used this to his full advantage and had his hands in my pockets from the first time when he laid his eyes on me.

I was young, ambitious, basically alone in the cold world, and starving for love. I was a cub trying to survive out in the wilderness and easy prey for any seasoned, savage beast. After luring me in through his temporary generosity of showering me with candy and flowers, I was entangled in his net of deception. He quickly became like a parasite that I couldn't extinguish. Within weeks, he moved in for the kill, manipulating me to let him move into my apartment, which was a gracious accommodation compared to the efficiency that he was living in. Shortly afterward, he quit his job to pursue some dream that promised overnight wealth. He was always looking for a get-rich-quick scheme. When he ran out of his own cash, he started borrowing money from me. He guilefully pushed my buttons of desire to succeed, convincing me to put up money on business ventures that went sour. Between my diligence and appetite for prosperity, I thought that I had the ingredients that bred success. Nevertheless, my shortsightedness in trusting him to handle any affairs that held the possibility of breaking free from him only ensured me that I would remain his prisoner. After all, he wasn't going to cut off the hand that was feeding him. When I discovered that he had been gambling and boozing it up with his buddies (his so-called business prospects), I stopped loaning him money.

Still, I allowed him to float on my back whenever he was in between jobs or whenever I was feeling lonely and vulnerable. Chronologically, I was sixteen years his junior. However, it was as though I became the parent who had to bear the responsibility of his survival. Night after night, I had dinner on the table waiting for him to come home. Hours later, I usually tracked him down at a local pub, where I would find him drunk, playing pinball, and smoking one cigarette after another. When I wised up a little and realized that he was more interested in cleaning whiskey bottles, I refused to remain his enabler. His need to find another way to continue indulging in his destructive devices eventually got him a job at the pub that he often frequented.

Century Village is also where I met Sophie Tettelbaum, my office manager. The half century that divided Sophie and I in age is what also brought us together and defined the essence of our relationship. One of the common threads we shared was that both our mothers died when we were young. She understood what it was like to be cast aside by a physically present but emotionally absent father for the sake of keeping peace in his second marriage. She also knew what it was like to be reminded by a stepmother that her needs and wants overshadowed any child's, especially a child who wasn't her own. Our needs secured a secret place in each other's hearts, where seeds of love were sprinkled and a line of nurture was created. We entrusted each other with our struggles, and the strength we found in sharing these made them easier to bear.

Besides teaching me how to play canasta, Sophie also taught me the art of coupon clipping. I learned where to find *billik vi borscht*, the best bargains as cheap as beet soup. I admired her for several reasons, but what I admired about her most was her zest for life. Though she had been widowed for many years, she didn't allow her age to stop her from living life to its fullest. When she wasn't working, she was doting over her family, socializing with friends, going to temple, or going halfway around the world exploring other countries and cultures. She was the first Jewish person I had ever met, and she introduced me to the warmth and commitment to family that the culture is known for.

Sophie detested laziness and anyone who traveled through life on a free ride, especially at the expense of those whose work went unnoticed and without rewards. She appreciated my hard work and diligent efforts, endearing me with the Yiddish idiom *yingeh tzahtzkeh* (a living doll), often boasting how I ran circles around the other clerk in our office, Tina. Sophie claimed that Tina was always carrying on as a *patsher*, doing her work in a half-ass manner. If she had her way, she said many times that she would eliminate the "dead weight" that took up our office space. I was hungry for a maternal figure's guidance, and I respected and cherished her kindness, wit, and wisdom. Along the way, I was taking mental notes as to how she handled herself and how she dealt with the public.

There were two doors to our office. Sophie's desk was in the reception area, where she greeted buyers, sellers, landlords, and tenants. If a landlord or tenant got out of hand and Tina and I couldn't handle them, then we would send them to the front, where Sophie would diffuse the situation. Because the office I shared with Tina was in the back of the building, Sophie was like the watchdog. When an irate tenant or landlord was coming to chew us out—during the time it took them to leave her office and walk to ours—she would warn us by calling us on the telephone. She also personally saved my butt on more than one occasion.

After the season was over and most of the snowbirds had gone home, our office was like a morgue. It was hard to keep busy or make it appear as if we were.

Harold (the boss and broker) often caught all of us playing cards or board games in the back office. During those slow periods, I had a difficult time staying alert and sometimes drifted off after lunch. When Harold caught me, he considered firing me. Tina played office politics well and was *a toches-lecker*. (Her lipstick was always on his behind.) But unlike her, I couldn't talk my way out of trouble, so Sophie stepped in and saved me.

Besides being prudent with her finances, Sophie also knew how to increase them. This inevitably rubbed off on me, and she encouraged me to increase my income by suggesting that I clean the vacant apartments before they were occupied again. Therefore, I decided to quit working for the real estate office and venture out on my own. The decision to clean residences on a full-time basis doubled my income within a matter of months. And even though Sophie and I no longer worked together, we promised to keep in touch.

5

Evan's embrace held me emotionally hostage. The image of our last interlude faithfully danced, waning in slow currents up to my memory banks. I dwelt on his reaction weeks earlier when I went to pick up Jim's dry cleaning. I reasoned that if he didn't care and had no feelings for me, then his reaction would have been different. I entertained his previous notion of marriage. Thus, the fantasy was born to win him over and get him back. The transition wouldn't happen overnight; yet I had little time to waste.

The first step was to go back to school. An area of interest to me was the field of architecture. I was relatively good at drawing and liked to be creative. After checking out the community college and finding out that most of the courses that I needed to take were during the day, I opted for a technical school. The school had an excellent track record and offered job placement assistance. In their eighteen-month program (with no summer break), I would be attending classes three nights a week. Upon completion, I would earn an associate's degree in architectural drafting.

The second step was to get rid of Jim. I had to be clever where he was concerned, because for once I needed him for something constructive. Although the cleaning helped me support myself, I hadn't been declaring most of my income. I didn't have documented proof of the adequate income that was necessary to qualify for a school loan that would cover the entire tuition. This meant that half the tuition could be paid with a grant and the other half with a school loan. That's where Jim came into the picture. I needed him to sign a statement declaring that he had been supporting me for the last year. This was a lie, of course, but my back was up against the wall. I did feel guilty about having him lie for me. But I knew the payoff would be more beneficial to the government when I earned my degree, started working for a company, and was able to pay *all* of my taxes. Then I would definitely be contributing to the system. Besides, it wasn't my fault that Father grossed an income that was close to six figures for the past several years but failed to provide anything beyond the essentials, including not saving for his children's college education.

Although Jim was initially supportive about my decision to go back to school, I didn't need him around draining my energy or bank account. I knew that once he noticed that I was exuding self-assurance and striving for a better quality of life that didn't include him, he would resort to more oppressive tactics. He was a gifted artist who exhibited the talents to create chaotic masterpieces at my expense. He could drown in his own pool of psychosis, but he wasn't taking me with him. I needed to reserve my strength in order to continue cleaning full time and attend classes at night. As soon as I got his signature, I broke off our engagement. I gave him two weeks to find another crib to crawl into.

Sophie was tickled when I told her that I had decided to go back to school and had broken up with Jim. So, as she was bringing a close to the Sabbath on a late Saturday afternoon, she invited me over for dinner to celebrate my emancipation.

She smeared a spoonful of chopped herring salad over a chunk of challah bread. "So you're finally getting rid of that *luftmentsh*."

"What's that?" I spread some chopped liver on a cracker.

"A man who builds castles in the air but never achieves anything," Sophie said.

"The sooner he gets out of my life, the better off I'll be. By this time next week, he should be gone."

"Only this time don't take him back, no matter how much he says he'll change," Sophie said. "A leopard never changes his spots. Maybe with Jim out of the way, you and Evan can get back together."

I smiled. "That thought has crossed my mind. But I do think you're partial to Evan because he's Jewish."

"I can only say from experience of spending forty years with my beloved Sol, *olov hasholem* [may he rest in peace], Jewish men make great husbands. Have you heard from the *mentsh* lately?"

"No. Besides, if I want anything serious with Evan, he already warned me about the rejection I'd get from his family. Well . . . at least his grandparents, which are who he's going to be living with while he's going to Nova."

"He can always find another place to stay, and his grandparents aren't going to live forever. His parents are the ones you need the approval from. Once they get know you, they'll warm up to you." She raised one of her eyebrows as she said, "Anyway, a *goyeh* can always convert to Judaism if she wants to."

We went into the kitchen, and I helped her put the roasted chicken, noodle kugel, and cucumber salad on the dining room table. By the time we finished eating dinner, my belly was full and so was my heart. I was more determined than ever to reach for the stars.

When I returned home later that evening around ten o'clock and noticed Jim's car parked in front of Lauren's house, a knot of unease formed in the pit of my stomach. Saturday nights were usually a long night for bartenders, so I wasn't expecting him home until hours later. My throat tightened, and I struggled to breathe evenly. As I walked up the driveway and passed Lauren's living room windows, I began to realize that there were no lights on in my apartment, nor were the porch lights on. I fumbled in the dark for my keys. After I unlocked the deadbolt to the front door, I couldn't get the door open. Apparently, Jim had secured the inside latch, making it impossible for me to get in.

I knocked loudly on the door. "Jim, open up." When he didn't respond, I walked over to the bedroom window and tapped on it. "Jim, wake up! I can't get in!"

I suddenly heard glass shattering, followed by the crash of an object hitting a wall. I watched his raging shadow split my wooden kitchen table and chairs into shreds and smash my glass living room tables into pieces.

Within minutes, Lauren came outside through the back door of her sun porch. Fortunately, her daughters were sleeping over at their grandmother's and were not present to see the monster in action. "What's going on?" she asked.

"When I got home, he wouldn't let me inside."

Amid his tirade, we heard him ranting and raving but couldn't understand what he was saying. "I'm calling the police," she said. I started to walk over to the front door of my apartment. "Stay away from there. He's going crazy right now, and he'll only hurt you."

I followed her into her house, where she called the police. As Jim's fury continued, he picked up anything his mighty madness strengthened him with and threw it against the walls. The police officers arrived twenty minutes later. As soon as they asked him to come out and face them, he started shouting obscenities at them. When they threatened to use force if necessary, he opened the door. His hands were cut and bleeding, and he *acted* like he was totally out of it. While one of the officers went inside to check out the damage, the other officer forced him down to the ground and tried to restrain him. Jim sobbed, pounded his fist on the pavement, and kicked his legs as if he were a two-year-old who was having a tantrum. While the first officer quickly came back outside and placed handcuffs on him, the other officer read him his rights.

Lauren and I were sitting on the porch steps, facing the courtyard that separated her house and my apartment. Before they took Jim away, I approached him. "It's really over this time. If anything happens to my car or to me, the police will know who did it and they'll be looking for you."

Lauren stood up and stated frankly, "You're no longer welcome here, so have someone else come back to get your things."

I was relieved that he had brought physical damage to material possessions that could be replaced. Yet I was unhappy that it took him minutes to demolish what it had taken me three years to accrue. My angst lessened when I realized that I was finally exterminating the parasite that had been feeding off me for the past two years.

In the days that followed, I was making the adjustment of functioning on six hours of sleep a night.

Existing on large amounts of espresso helped me settle into a routine of rising early to study and work on my drawings, put in a full day of work, and then attend classes at night. It took a while to hand over the reins of freedom that I had enjoyed before—like setting my own schedule—and resign to a more structured format. On the other hand, if I had been working for someone other than myself, I wouldn't have been allowed the luxury of a flexible schedule. I invited the exhaustion and stayed focused on my reward.

I had no desire to see Jim. He could've fallen off the face of the earth, and I wouldn't have noticed or cared. But parasites are hard to kill, especially when you've been infested with them for so long. Just when you think you've gotten rid of all the remnants of their existence, they show up again, uninvited, plotting a more insidious manner to plague their prey. To avoid future infestations, sometimes several toxic treatments are necessary to ensure that they don't return—Jim was no exception.

He called and requested a meeting with me. He apologized for his behavior that night, blaming it on tainted cocaine, which he claimed that a coworker had given him. He said that he wanted to pay me back the two thousand dollars that he had owed me. When I refused, aware that he had no resources to come up with any extra money, he taunted me further. "I think it's in your best interest that you meet with me. Don't worry, I'm not going to hurt you."

"Don't play games with me. Just tell me over the phone."

"Stop over at the pub before you go to school tonight. I take my dinner break around five o'clock. If you want to finish school and get your degree, you'll be here."

45

As I walked through the parking lot of the pub, I chewed the skin around the cuticles of my fingernails. I was ready for anything but uncertain of what to expect. I entered the patio and passed the customers who surrounded the outside bar. Blue tarp awnings flapped with the winds from the coast. The confusing chambers of my head vibrated in between the loud music. The cigarette smoke added to my lightheadedness and contributed to my nausea. I treaded with tremor and walked stiffly up the planks of stairs that joined the patio bar and inside lounge.

When Jim saw me approach the bar, he smirked like a hungry lion who was about to devour a side of beef. Immediately, he directed me back outside and into the parking lot. I hesitated to follow him but then realized it was happy hour. People would be passing through the parking lot. So if he tried to attack me, there would be witnesses. I knew that he had better sense than to jeopardize his job, especially since I was no longer around to pick up the pieces when he tumbled.

He walked over to his car. As he reached inside for his briefcase, the beads of sweat on my forehead multiplied. He had his back turned away from me, and I was getting ready to run. When he took out an envelope and handed it to me, my heart resumed its natural rhythm. "What's this?" I asked.

The stench of scotch fused his words together. He replied with cockiness, "Open it and find out." He had composed a letter addressed to the U.S. Department of Education. It stated that I had lied on my application and that I had been operating a cleaning business under the table, cheating the government out of their taxes. I misjudged his intelligence, not thinking that he was smart enough to know that it was considered a federal felony to lie on school loan and grant applications. He threatened, "I'm going to send this to them. You're going to have to pay all that money back, and you're going to prison. You can't just kick me out of your life and expect not to pay."

"You don't scare me anymore. I've moved on, and just being around you again makes me want to vomit." I ripped up the letter, letting the tales of trickery float and scatter onto the pavement.

There was an air of certainty in his voice. "Don't worry, I have copies."

"Good!" I fired back. "Oh, and if you don't have the proper address to send that letter to, I would be more than willing to get it for you. I meant what I said—*it's over*. I can't keep carrying you!" I walked away and never experienced the displeasure of setting eyes on him again.

6

I was baby-sitting Megan while Lauren and her other daughter were out at the movies. One of the things to do on our "little people's" agenda was to have a fashion show. We had gone through her closet and mine, picking out some blouses, hats, and shoes for her chic ensemble. I have always loved children and indulged in the pleasure of spending time with them. Whenever I'm in the presence of one of God's greatest gifts, not a care in the world exists.

I spoke into the toy microphone. "Ladies and gentlemen—oh, I mean boys and girls. It gives me great pleasure to present to you . . ." Before I continued to frolic in my role as host, I waited until she came out of her bedroom and began making her grand entrance down the hallway. "Chatelaine Megan. The shift she's wearing is from Petite's Parlor; her hat is from Dior's Darlings; and the flats she's parading in are from Little Leathers, imported all the way from Milan. Oh, and I just love that fragrance she's wearing. It's the new splash sensation, A La Baby." She giggled and batted her long, almond eyelashes.

When she got to the doorway of the bathroom, she stopped, as if on cue, and tipped the side of the wide-brimmed hat that buried her forehead. Then she turned around, paused, and gazed at her reflection in the full-length mirror that was hanging on the wall at the end of the hall. She licked her lips and asked, "Can I have some more lip stuff?"

I walked into the bathroom, brought out the tube of lip-gloss, and handed it to her. The tenderberry silk frost brought out the cobalt-blue crystals in her eyes. After she dabbed some on her lips, she licked them and repeated the process. I leaned down and squatted on my knees. "Silly girl, you're not supposed to eat it."

"It smells like berries." She held it up to my nose. "See."

"Okay. I think it's time for a makeup break." For the next hour, we plastered layers of makeup on each other's face and painted each other's fingernails. After her bath and while we laid in bed, I read her a bedtime story.

When I finished, she asked, "Where's Jim?"

"I'm not sure."

"Is he coming back?"

"No," I said.

"So who's going to stay with you now?"

"Nobody."

"Aren't you scared?" she asked.

"Sometimes."

"Why can't your daddy and mommy come and stay with you?"

"Because I'm all grown up. Besides, my daddy snores so loud that the whole house shakes."

She picked her head up off the pillow. "Not ah."

"Yeaha." I raised my eyebrows and opened my eyes wide. "One time he was snoring so loud that somebody who lived across the street called the police."

She put her hand up to her mouth. "Um. They took him to jail."

"They were going to send him to jail for disturbing the peace, but then they changed their minds."

"What's distur—peace mean?"

"Making a lot of noise. You know—like when I do this." She laughed as I began to tickle her.

She retaliated by pinching me. I was wearing an oversized T-shirt, so the only exposed skin was on my arms and thighs. When she caught her breath, she grabbed some skin on my thighs and pointed to the cellulite, then asked, "How come your legs have those things?"

I paused a moment before I answered. "Those are dimples. See, even my legs are happy to be spending time with a baby doll!" I went on to tickle her for a few more moments.

Then she asked, "Do you love another honey?"

"I think so."

I made the mistake in piquing the interest of her precocious mind. "Who is it?"

"You ask too many questions. Now let's get some sleep." I tucked her in and went to sleep on the other canopy bed, which was on the other side of the fruitwood dresser that separated the beds.

After a few minutes, she was standing at my bedside, holding her doll and receiving blanket. She looked at me, shrugged her shoulders, and then asked timidly, "Well?"

"Oh all right." I pretended to sigh. "But don't hog all the covers."

"You better not snore and make us go to jail," she ordered.

"Yes ma'am."

While I became tranquilized by the sound of her breathing, I started realizing why I had hung onto someone who was so bad for me for so long. I was beginning to understand the dangerous repercussions in being a casualty of the daddy deficit. His recent rejection was invading my cells like a terminal ailment.

50

I replayed the scenes over in my head of what had transpired over the last several weeks.

I had spent hardly any time with Father after I left home. This was his choice—not mine—particularly once he learned that Jim and I had been living together without being married. Even so, I made a few attempts to reach out to him, periodically sending him a greeting card. When I didn't get a response, I wondered if he even received them since Helen was usually home—and the first one to get the mail.

I didn't miss Helen or Father much. But I did miss my younger siblings and tried to stay in contact with them. At least once a month, I would take them somewhere to socialize. So when I learned that Helen was out of town visiting relatives, I invited Father and them over for dinner. I had a glimmer of hope that once I invited him into my home and he saw how responsible I had become, he would give me the respect that I didn't get as a child. I was looking for a way to reach out to him and possibly have the kind of relationship that fathers are known to have with their daughters.

He seemed impressed with my knack for decorating and commented, "This place is small, but you've done a wonderful job making the most out of the space. It's cute." Then he went on to commend my culinary skills when he asked for seconds. "You're a good cook like Rachel and Julia. They make everything from scratch, too."

After dinner, we went to a park that was close to my apartment. As we walked along the jogging path, he looked over toward the hospital across the street. "I remember coming here when Casandra was in the hospital dying," he stated.

This was the only time I ever remembered his bringing up the subject of Mom's death voluntarily. "How long was she in the coma before she died?" It was sad that my own mother was a stranger to me. It was sadder that even as an adult I had to refer to her as one, simply because of all the years that Helen's jealousy ruled his emotions.

"Three days." He went on to reminisce for several minutes, recalling what took place in the days before and the days following her death. His eyes became glassy. Keeping in mind what relatives had told me about my bearing an uncanny resemblance to Mom, I contemplated the notion that being in my presence might have caused memories about her to surface. Just the idea that he felt comfortable enough to share them with me encouraged me to take the next step.

I mentioned the cards that I had sent and asked him why he never responded. "You've been living with a man, and you're not married," he explained.

"Yes, but that was before. You saw for yourself; we broke up, and he moved out."

"I know," he said. "But you still committed fornication, which is a sin and could get you disfellow-shiped."

Disfellowshiping is a public ostracizing where an elder reads a formal letter to the congregation and identifies the person by name. At which point, no Witnesses—including the immediate family—are permitted to associate with this person. If any are caught doing so, they risk getting disfellowshiped themselves. In the interim, the degradation continues when the disfellow-shiped person is shunned when they enter into a room of other Witnesses. They are to be treated as if they are dead. The only time any family member, whose a Witness, can contact them is if there's a medical emergency or a death in the family. The only shot of redemption or only way this process can be altered is if the person shows repentance, continues to practice the religion, and doesn't miss a meeting. Then after a period of time, which is solely dependent upon the discretion of the elders, the person may be reinstated and welcomed back into the congregation.

Father went on to state that if I wrote a letter to the elders and confessed of my sin and showed repentance by going back to the meetings, he wouldn't hesitate to have a relationship with me. Thus, like a naive and loyal servant, I did what he requested, thinking that I was going to win his approval and eventually be able to share some bond with him. After which, I made myself scarce and tried to avoid a confrontation with him. I was hoping that he would forget about the letter, especially since I had decided that if I was excommunicated I wasn't going to try to get back into the fold. Because I had attended a different con-gregation briefly after I left home, I was hoping that Father wouldn't find out that I hadn't been attending any meetings. Unfortunately, what made our worlds collide was when I went to apply for financial aid at the school. Just as I was at Jim's mercy and needed him to say that he had been supporting me, I was at Father's mercy as well. Copies of previous tax returns, along with his signature to prove that he hadn't been declaring me as a dependent, were being requested. Without these, I wouldn't get the assistance that I needed. A couple of unanswered telephone calls left me no other alternative but to face Father again on his own turf.

Father was in his bedroom, sitting in a wingback leather chair and behind a large, oak desk, the top of which was buried under piles of bills and religious propaganda. I stood in front of him while Helen was reclined on the bed. She turned down the volume on her forty-two-inch projection television. *She was still playing the lead in the Broadway production of Helen Keller. She was acting her way into a Tony award nomination for her efforts to command attention, laying claim to being legally blind.*

"So you want to go to college," Father said. "What are you going to study?"

"I'm going for a degree in architectural drafting and design."

"You want to become an architect?" he asked.

"In the long run, yes. For now, though, I just want to get the drafting degree so that I can start working in the field as soon as possible. Then if I like it and do well, I'll pursue it further."

Father snickered while rolling his eyes. "That's a man's field. What makes you think you'll make it?"

"Times are changing," I replied with determination.

"You're right about times changing. Like the book of Revelation reveals, we're living with the signs that the end is near. Armageddon is just around the corner." When I didn't respond, he said, "Well, hon, I'm sorry that you wasted the trip."

"What do you mean?"

"I thought that you were going to call back when I got home from work . . . like Helen said."

"I tried, but the line was busy."

Helen saw me glance over at the telephone that was on top of the nightstand. The receiver was on its side. "Oh, I must have forgotten to hang it up after we finished dinner," she said.

"My accountant is out of town and won't be back until next week," Father stated. "He has all the copies of my tax returns."

"But by then I'll miss the application deadline for this semester."

Helen interrupted, "What's another semester? It's your own fault for waiting until the last minute."

"The loan officer at the school said she mailed out a letter a few weeks ago."

Father scratched his head and said, "Well, I never got it."

My experience with Helen had taught me that she was one of the last persons who wanted to see me succeed. I concluded that the first letter, which requested all the necessary information, probably wound up in the trash.

I was getting exasperated, but I couldn't show him and empower him with any more ammunition. I needed to get what I came for. He had robbed me of so much in my life; I wasn't going to let him steal the only opportunity I had left to get a higher education. "Will you at least sign off on this letter that states that you haven't been supporting me?"

He signed the letter, but he was going to be sure to brand me with a more punishing signature. "By the way, did you ever get around to writing a letter to the elders of your congregation?"

"Yes, and I mailed it to them."

I fell into Father's trap without feeling the grip of the vise tighten. In that moment, it had become obvious to me that he had apparently been preparing for my execution for a while, laying the insidious groundwork in our previous visit. I was like a lamb being led to the slaughter by a shepherd's hands that were bloodstained with hypocrisy. I felt like I was eight years old again, being summoned into their bedroom to get a spanking. I stared blankly out of the bay window toward the forest behind the backyard, where I often went as a child to retreat among the Florida dogwood, holly, ficus, and eucalyptus trees. The chains of captivity, which their psychosis kept me bound in, were still dangling from my neck as I began to feel trapped.

"So none of the elders have contacted you?" he asked.

"No," I said timidly while my mind drifted further away.

He immediately called and briefly spoke to one of the elders. He rose out of his chair, off his atoning throne, and stood erect. I pictured his brainwashed subordinate clicking the counters of his boots together in unison with his dictator. The devoted follower approved the final orders for an execution that my own father had instigated.

When Father hung up the receiver of the telephone, content that his strategic plan to exult judgment upon his foe was a success, he said, "They decided to disfellowship you. They read the letter and informed the congregation a few weeks ago. But if you'd been attending the meetings like you said you were, you would've already known." He sneered disdainfully, "You know what that means. See what happens when you turn your back on Jehovah. No degree is going to save you when Armageddon comes."

"What about Jack?" I asked.

"Jack has nothing to do with this," Helen said.

"He got Donna, who is only fourteen years old, pregnant."

Helen defended him. "They got married."

"Yes," I said, "but he committed fornication with her before they got married."

"Jack was never baptized—you were," Father said.

He might as well have marked me on my forehead and threw me into exile. I walked out of the bedroom without saying another word. As I passed through the family room, I whispered to Kara, Beth, and Kate. "I'll have to sneak to see you guys."

I knew that I would be denied of even seeing any of my siblings who were living under Father's roof. While some of the remaining siblings wouldn't deny me, the ones who were still under the influence of the cult would. I got in my car and cranked up the volume on the radio.

Music was the vehicle that helped me escape bondage temporarily during my teenage years. I would sit in dark seclusion in the living room (which was off limits, except when guests came to visit), with the volume on the stereo turned down low. The lyrics clamored my silent screams of entrapment—in what I considered to be a childhood prison camp. Occasionally, as Father prepared a snack from the kitchen and I didn't get to the stereo fast enough to turn it off, the sound would attract his attention. He would come into the dining room (which was in between the kitchen and the living room) and turn on the light. He would've had to have been blind not to notice my tears. He never questioned what was behind them or my sorrow. He simply made his snack and went back to his own cell.

Though I had fled his cribbed prison, I remained his hostage, where the only institution was the one inside my mind. And now, added to my collection of the blues, were songs of fury that played upon my tarnished soul. The squall of his failure to acknowledge my existence created a gaping hole inside of me that gushing waterfalls could not fill. I had to swallow the bitter pill of acceptance. Father was not going to give up his method to overpower me, and I wasn't going to wave any flag of defeat and surrender my immunity to exercise independent thinking. Instead of looking behind I looked ahead, knowing that it would be years, if ever, before I saw him again.

Fashionable preparations were winding down. I had spent the last two weekends going to garage sales and sifting through rummage in consignment shops. I found an antique wicker set and divider that separated my small living quarters quaintly. I painted all the pieces pearl white and trimmed them with rose accents, which welcomed the pale rose flat finish that I shaded the walls with.

The following Monday, early morning clouds were sweating gently. I sat, getting dizzy from the espresso I was sipping and intoxicated by the fragrance that was permeating the air. The gardenia bush outside the kitchen window was drinking in the droplets that settled into their satin petals, preparing itself for the first dance of spring. I thought about what words I would use to capture my beloved's heart. I couldn't decide what I was going to tell Evan first: that I had gone back to school or that I had broken off my engagement.

I was transforming myself into an educated counterpart without the support of anyone. The disconcert that Evan might have felt, along with the need to conceal me from his family, would be replaced with pride, especially once he learned that I was willing to convert to Judaism. And I would be determined to raise our children in the same traditions, keeping true to their heritage. I was not only seeking his approval but his family's as well. I was no longer just a maid who wasn't worthy of their son's love and would tarnish their family image. By the time my transformation was complete, there wouldn't be any reason left to treat me as an outsider. I would be welcomed as any other mate would. Yes—I thought—I will make them forget that I was never born a Jew.

I couldn't deny or suppress my feelings any longer, nor could I waste any more time. So on my way to work, I made a detour, hoping to catch Evan and invite him over for dinner later that night or sometime during the week. When I got to the building, everything was locked up, and no one was in sight. I figured that he wasn't open for business yet or he was out making a delivery or pickup. I scribbled a quick note and asked him to he call me. I thought about leaving it in the door but then changed my mind. When I remembered what day it was and that Lauren usually did her laundry on Mondays, I returned home. Lauren agreed to give Evan or Daniel the note without mentioning anything else.

I went to work, barely able to concentrate on my duties and exuberantly anticipated the hours that were ahead. I finished cleaning one house and had more than an hour to spare before I was expected at the second one. Though I never went home for lunch, I felt strongly compelled to do so that day. I assumed it was my impatience to learn if Evan got my note and what his response was. I scurried home and was pleased to notice Lauren's car in the driveway. She must have noticed me pass by her living room windows because she met me at my front door. "Did you give him the note?" I asked excitedly.

Lauren stumbled with her words. "You . . . you better sit down."

It felt like my heart had dropped to my feet. "What is it?" I asked.

"I have some really bad news."

My anxiety wouldn't let her continue. "Did he get into an accident? Oh, no, don't tell me he's marrying that girl."

As tears welled up in her eyes, she nodded. "No, that's not it." Then they slowly erupted down her face. "There's no easy way to say this. He . . . he committed suicide over the weekend."

"What?" I gasped. "How?"

"Apparently they found him in his bedroom. He had been drinking and shot himself in the heart."

I stood in numb disbelief. My legs became pillars that fixed themselves firmly into the foundation of my tragedy. My mind shut down, creating a barrier to any rationale or raw emotion. Inside my dazed confusion, I mumbled, "I have to see him."

"You can't. His funeral was this morning."

"I have to get out of here."

"Honey wait. Please don't go. You're not okay, and you shouldn't be alone right now." But I was back in my car and gone before she could catch me.

I drove around for hours, with every street turning into a maze of haziness. In my quandary, I went over to his villa. *He's in there. I know it. Evan, Daniel, Lauren—they're all playing a joke on me.* I saw his car in the parking lot. I rang the doorbell. Silence. I knocked loudly on the door. *I know you're in there, Evan.* When I realized that the whole world of illusion I had created was crumbling beneath me, I finally slumped down on the landing of the stairs.

The days that followed brought inclement weather, which seemed so befitting to the deluge of tears that ensued. I couldn't get the imprint of Evan's face out of my mind. As I put on the flannel overcoat, which he had insisted that I keep, I lingered in the faded scent of his cologne. Only now there was no warmth inside it, only cold emptiness. Every man whom I saw wearing a baseball cap reminded me of the Yankees cap that he wore. I followed them. But when they turned around and I saw their face, I was inflicted with the blows of cruel reality once more.

No amount of sunshine could brighten the dark well of my soul. Nor could the winds of change deflect the arrow of death that pierced through my heart. In desperate hopes to wash away my sorrow, I stood in the shower and let the water beat against my flesh. My limp body curled into a ball of grief. I released my sobs into the same river of agony he must have been in when he lost his faith.

In my despair, I reached out for something to hold on to—anything that could keep me from sliding off the edge of the hopeful universe that I had started to create for myself. Before I plunged into a black abyss, the powers above heard my call. They sent a vessel of light to my door, and an angel caught my fall.

Enfolded in the loving arms of Sophie is where I fell. She enchanted my ears by reciting the Mourners' Kaddish. I hung on to the only comfort I could find in the melody that she sang in the only way she knew how. She then reminded me that there was a blessing in every tragedy; although in those days and for many that followed, I felt cursed. I was certain I was getting punished for the filthy sinner Father accused me of being. The blood boiled beneath my skin with an angry flame toward God. I was a smoldering ember of regret. Evan's legacy of pain that had taken harbor inside my womb was now fighting for its life. As I listened to the last selection on the cassette "Careless Whisper" repeatedly, I wept in song.

Lost without its drummer boy, the strings of my

heart were silenced. It would be a few years before my eyes began to drift and my heart began to beat to a different drummer.

7

From the moment that I picked up the receiver and recognized the voice on the other end of the line, my internal panic switch sounded, warning me of another foray. The enemy was moving in for a major kill. The forces of evil weren't satisfied in taking out every ally in the surrounding territories of my world. In efforts to shatter every dream I ever had, it wanted more. Apparently, it was now on a mission to destroy me physically.

The conversation had ended minutes before, but my hand was frozen on the receiver. The nurse's voice still shrilled inside my ears. "This is Connie at Dr. Epstien's office. The results on your MRI are in. Is your husband there with you?"

"My husband's at work."

"Can you get in touch with him?"

"Why?"

"The doctor wants both of you to come in to the office as soon as possible."

"It's bad news, isn't it?"

"Dr. Epstein will discuss the results with you when you come in."

My mind went numb and was looking to escape from reality and fade into fantasy. I was standing trial, waiting for the verdict to be handed down. I was not ready to receive a death sentence, nor was I prepared to count down my hours until expiration. The time was here. The demons I had grown up with had come to claim what was theirs. I pictured them dancing with delight at their conquest. And it was all because the greatest transgression had taken place: the crime of cravings and desires so deep that sent my soul searching for someone to love and someone who would love me in return. I had been looking for the unconditional warmth and acceptance I had experienced with Nana when I was a child. Between the fleeting time I had with her, being motherless, and having Father deny me on every level, I had become lovelorn. I was willing to sacrifice whatever I had or do whatever it took to satisfy those hunger pangs deep inside. At last, I, a lonely little girl for most of my life, had found my rendition of a prince.

I drifted in a daze and watched the midday sun dance upon the surface of the swimming pool that was just beyond the sliding glass doors. The sheets of glass covering the surface of the water mirrored autumn, a season of paradise in the Sunshine State. I opened one of the sliders, stared up at the sapphire sky, and felt the tropical breezes that were swaying in perfect sync with nature. I took a scenic inventory of my backyard sanctuary.

The last of the lilies had bloomed for the season. Their trumpet petals were bidding farewell, blowing in orange contrast behind the crimson leaves and green caladium that bordered the perimeter of the screened enclosure. A blue jay was guarding her nest that was deep within the branches of the black-olive tree, which shaded the green carpet of grass leading to the edge of the pond. The delicate, sweet scent of salmon and white petunias that I had planted in between blue and purple pansies attracted a family of ducks. The mother came up out of the pond with her ducklings trailing behind. While the petals from the petunias tickled her ducklings' beaks, she nestled them.   Everywhere I looked, I saw creation.

I walked to the guestroom, a temporary surrogate for the nursery that I had planned when my husband, Arthur, and I felt comfortable in starting a family. I intentionally painted the walls a chartreuse green to adapt to either sex of our baby, and he framed the windows and ceiling with crown moldings. I walked over to the dresser and stared at the picture of Arthur when he was a toddler.   He looked so soft and innocent as a little boy.   I set the picture down and picked up the gift that his mother, Ilona, had given me the first time we met.   My fingers tingled as they brushed against the red velvet canvas and outlined the raised, bronze silhouette of the Madonna and her child. Then I swayed back and forth in the rocking chair that was next to the windows.   I had never entertained the possibility of our time together being cut so short.   I thought that many years lay ahead for us, and a future with children was just that: in the distant future.   I was tilling and testing the soil in the marriage before I planted the seed, never imagining that in the spring of our love, the harvest would become barren because of the fall of my fairy tale dreams.

My heart also wept in anguish regret when I realized what I had thrown away some years ago.   At the age of twenty-six, I was sorry for aborting Evan's baby so that I could continue with school and start a career.   I always felt that if I had carried the baby to term I would've had a girl.   I didn't want her to be an object of rejection and to measure her merit by her father's absence and my emotional abandonment.   Just as Father ignored my cries, I ignored my baby's silent pleas.   While I was there to complain about my existence, I gave her no say in the matter.   I imagined how old *she* would've been and how the sound of her laughter could enchant my ears. With that, her giggles directed my attention toward the window. I watched her image jump through the shower of sprinklers that were watering the grass in the backyard. She seemed to be doing her best to get wet. I was convinced that she had come to take me home and the three of us would be a family in another world.

I watched my reflection on the windowpane turn into hers. She put her nose up to the soft, pink petals of the *Luculia gratissima* shrubs that were next to the window; she inhaled their magnetic fragrance. Then she put her palms flat up to the pane of glass as if she wanted to touch me. I placed my palms against the windowpane to meet hers. But as soon as our hands met, I was back in reality.

I retreated briefly to the den, a place that Arthur considered his refuge. It was one of the few rooms in the house where I waived my decorating rights. While sitting in the overstuffed wing-back chair, I scanned the library of books (history novels, aircraft illustrations, and all the disciplines of engineering) that filled two bookcases. Models of military aircraft, antique cars, and ships were displayed on shelves that were on either side of the bookcases. As I thought about all the literary masterpieces I had never taken the time to read because I was too busy creating my own Shakespearean tragedy, my eyes were wet with tears. Before long, *she* was standing in front of me. Her tiny finger followed the tears that trailed down my cheeks.

She took my hand and led me to the other side of the house and into the master bedroom. I laid on the bed where Arthur and I indulged in intimate pleasures, wondering how it was ever going to be the same after this. If I got lost under the covers of the past, I would never want to face whatever horror was looming. *She* had been standing at the foot of the bed, and she knelt down to pray. When I got up, she gestured for me to join her in petition, but my animosity toward God kept me standing. I had no desire to kneel before God and the crucifix that was hanging over the bed, for I thought it was pointless to pray for a miracle that I was certain would never take place. Just as I thought I had the power to make my baby girl appear in spirit, I wished that I had the power to hurl the menacing monster, who was threatening to take over my body, out the window and into the pond. But I knew that there was no magic wand that could make the poison inside of my body vanish.

After I called Arthur at work, I walked into the living room, where I waited for him to come home. I opened the front door. The breeze blowing through the screen door invited the perfume from the love-in-a-mist fennels that were hanging in the air. I stood next to the bay window and admired the violet-blue and lemon-yellow autumn crocus, which seemed to be reaching up to greet me. The oleander shrubs that were on either side of the crocus bed were in full bloom. The queen palms that Arthur had planted when we first moved into the house were growing rapidly. They added a neat touch to the spotlessly manicured front lawn. Though at times it drove me crazy, his demand for neatness and order was praiseworthy.

The recurring dizziness that I had been suffering from for the past two weeks forced me to brace myself against the fireplace. I turned on the synthetic logs and collapsed onto the fluffy cushions of the sofa. I reasoned that because I had just received what I believed was the call of death, my mind was playing tricks on me. The stressful obsession that the worst was yet to come, and that I was having hallucinations as a result, was exhausting. My eyes blinked heavily, and the feign crackling sound from the synthetic logs in the fireplace hypnotized me further. I felt the afghan, which Ilona had crocheted for us, being pulled over my body. After *she* covered me, she caressed my head, and I settled into a deep sleep.

My dream state carried me back in time to when Arthur and I met. It was a time when I never imagined that the genie of love would grant me another wish, and that someone else could spark the passion inside of me that I thought had died with Evan.

8

After feeling abandoned again when Evan decided to end his life, the last thing on my mind was falling in love or getting seriously involved with any man. Eventually, my heart resumed a steady beat. The tremors, due to the aftershock of his sudden death, ceased. My body stopped trembling in fear of what Jim was going to do for revenge. My cognitive abilities returned, and I found comfort in the distraction of my studies. I poured my pain into my architectural drawings and renderings, where the rooms flowed with creative ease. My daily routine gave me the structure I was familiar with growing up, always having an authoritative figure telling me what to do and when to do it. The talent and freedom to create within these boundaries nurtured my artistic side. It was the first time in my life that I took pride in how I earned a living. When I graduated and saw my name on the degree printed in bold letters, I beamed with self-confidence.

It was 1988 when I landed my first job as a computer draftsperson. I was a subcontractor in the Facilities Division at IBM. Getting my foot in the door of a major corporation was a milestone for me in more ways than one. The backaches from leaning over a drafting table; the calluses from holding a drafting pencil; and the eyestrain from manipulating rulers, triangles, and compasses for hours on end were finally beginning to pay off. It felt good to be working in a field that wasn't physically demanding and one where I was able to utilize my brain cells instead of having them evaporate with the cleaning solutions. The simple pleasure, of being able to draw in fresh air and breathe a sigh of relief that my days of hell were behind me, gave me a new perspective on what direction I wanted my life to take. That is, until I met Arthur Concha, a man whose very presence took my breath away.

Though the projects that I worked on in the beginning usually entailed only basic revisions and little interaction with the engineers, the software system was completely foreign and intimidating to me. Since it wasn't commonly used in the engineering field and it wasn't the program that I was taught in school, it took me a few weeks to get acclimated with it. Arthur was a facility designer who shared an office with other designers and project engineers. However, in his office he worked strictly from hard copies and a drafting table. So when he needed to create drawings or make revisions onto the database system, he had to use an available computer in my office or one nearby. In order to assist me through the learning curve, he made himself conveniently available on a daily basis.

Even though I was physically attracted to him, the wedding band on his finger made him off limits. His arrogance, and the fact that he bragged endlessly about his material possessions, turned me off. But I felt drawn to him because in some ways he reminded me of Evan. He had dark hair, was average height, did weight training religiously, and occasionally smoked cigars. Before long, I found myself accepting his invitations to join him and his two male coworkers for lunch. It was awhile before I recognized that his interest in me went beyond the boundaries of a coworker.

It took a male colleague, who was also married and having an affair with someone on the other side of the building, to convince me. "Wake up! Do you really think he's asking you how many kids you want and what you look for in a man because he wants to set you up with his younger brother?"

"That's what he says."

"Right. And I'm really Tom Cruise doing research for my next role. He wants you. I can see it in his eyes."

I smiled bashfully. "Even if that's the case, I don't date married men."

Although books had become my companions for the past few years, they paled in comparison to the highs and lows that come with a relationship. The loneliness was everywhere: under my bed, in between the covers, stealing my mind, and filling my head. It didn't take long for the universe to test my integrity and make me eat my words.

One day, when Arthur had his friends conveniently make other plans for lunch, he asked me to join him at a park that was within minutes of the facility. After we were finished eating, he told me about the problems that he and his wife, Elaine, were having. In general, he focused more on their incompatibility than anything else. They both met in upstate New York and eventually fell in love. When he accepted the contract position with IBM and transferred to Florida, they broke off their engagement. Suddenly, he was in a strange town with no family or friends. His loneliness and her vulnerability resulted in their rekindling their relationship after her first visit to Florida. As soon as she found a job, she relocated, and they married shortly after.

His parents weren't pleased with his choice in a mate, particularly because she came from the other side of the tracks like I did. Thus, they skipped the formalities of a traditional wedding and settled for exchanging vows at the county courthouse. They renewed their vows in a small ceremony inside a Catholic Church on their second anniversary. Though neither of their families attended, his boss and a few friends did. Decorating their first home in Boca Raton and building a new life together made up for what they had left behind. Because Elaine had been in an automobile accident and had a lawsuit pending in her favor before they married, he discouraged her from starting a family until it was settled. Then she could have the luxury of staying home and not return to work until the children were in school. New construction was on the rise, and homebuilders were in competition to offer buyers a better lifestyle. After Elaine's lawsuit was settled and she received a considerable amount for her suffering, he couldn't resist the temptation to upgrade. Therefore, in little more than a year they sold their home, turned a healthy profit, and were under contract to have a larger home built in an upper-middle-class neighborhood. Since they were close to getting settled in and she was anxious to start a family, he was running out of excuses. He confessed that he was having second thoughts; and having met someone like me wasn't making it any easier.

On the drive back, I sensed that he was excitably tense. I moved closer to the edge of the bucket seat, toward the armrest that divided us. It was as if one of us was waiting for the other to make the first move, but neither one of us dared to touch the other. Finally, I said, "You have a very unusual last name. What's your ethnicity?"

"Hungarian, but I'm the first generation in my family to be born in the States."

"Interesting . . . tell me more."

"My parents fled Budapest during the Hungarian Revolution and came over with thousands of other immigrants to Ellis Island."

"Didn't that revolution take place in '56?" I asked.

"I see that you were one of the few who were paying attention in history class."

"Not really . . . I remember fighting the urge to fall asleep during all those documentaries."

"I know what you mean," he said.

"Do you have family over there?"

"A few aunts, uncles, and cousins are there. I've never been over there, but they tell us the economy is very bad. My two cousins are close to my age, and they still live with my aunt and uncle. Even though they have degrees, they can't find a good job. They say it cost almost a year's salary just to buy a TV."

"It makes me appreciate this country even more when I hear stories like this. I think we're so spoiled over here sometimes that we don't realize how good we've got it. Most of us are striving for happiness when people in countries like that are happy just to have a roof over their heads."

"You've got it."

"So how old are you?" I asked.

"Twenty-eight . . . and you?"

"Old enough."

"Okay, I won't press. I know it's not nice to ask a lady her age."

"I'm probably close to your wife's age," I said.

"No way. I doubt you're a day over twenty-one."

"How old is she?"

"Thirty-one," he answered.

"So you like older women."

We approached a stoplight. He looked over and smiled. He put his hand on my knee. "Not always."

I stirred in the seat. "Do you speak Hungarian?"

He took his hand off my knee. "Yes, I'm fluent in it."

"I'm impressed."

"Don't be. I can speak it pretty well, but I have a difficult time reading or writing it. Hungarian is all my mother spoke while we were growing up."

"Does she speak English?"

"She can hold a conversation with you as long as you keep it light."

"Will you teach me some phrases?" I asked.

"That can be arranged."

"I have to go take some measurements in building three," he said. "Is anyone expecting you back right away?"

"No . . . unless Dale [my immediate supervisor] comes looking for me."

"I'll cover for you."

After he took the measurements he needed, we got on the elevator. We both went to push the button for the third floor at the same time. He took my hand, and I felt the faint sprinkles of perspiration in his palm and on his lips as he kissed it. As the elevator made its ascent, he stole his first kiss from me, which sent the butterflies in my stomach sailing. When the elevator stopped at the third floor with an abrupt jolt, I saw my stargazed expression reflected in his eyes, and we struggled for a second to regain our senses.

He said, "*Elamulni.*"

"What?"

"It means to be bewildered. Your first lesson in my

native tongue."

"I think starry-eyed is a better description. That kiss was an unexpected surprise."

"A pleasant one I hope. Come with me." He seasoned his words with a dash of arrogance. "There's much more from where that came from." He led me down the hallway and into the stairway that was just off the cafeteria. There were a handful of workers taking a late lunch. I held his hand as he took me behind the stairwell. His hands were above my shoulders, braced against the wall. He asked with a whisper, "So what's your favorite sport?"

I pulled on his silk tie, drawing him closer to me. I could feel his slate-blue eyes penetrate me. "Just about any that gives me a high."

"Sounds like you like to play hard." I found his choice of words bewitching. His tongue met my mouth, which became an open well, taking all that his exciting potion offered. When I felt his rise against my thighs, we came up for air. As my hands made their way around his buttocks, he smothered my neck with a velvet scarf of kisses.

A door slammed, and our brief walk through the fire of desire was extinguished. We walked back to the building where our offices were. As he said good-bye to me and went inside his office, I saw a door to my future open and cupid pass through it. In between a few scattered moments of being productive, I spent the rest of the afternoon daydreaming.

We twirled our way through the next few weeks in a whirlwind of foreplay. We continued to steal kisses inside elevators and behind stairwells. During our rush-hour lunches, we gobbled down our food so that we could spend the rest of the time feasting on each other's caresses. In the shade, he rested his head on my lap, and I stroked his hair gently before he drifted off for a brief nap. Nearly a month passed before I decided to play the game of love with him in its entirety.

While Elaine was visiting her family in New York for the weekend, he invited me to watch him and his squadron march in a Memorial Day parade. (He was a member of a voluntary organization that offers rescue efforts for small aircraft and marine vessels when they're in distress.) Later that evening, he took me back to my apartment. "So *szeretett enyem.*" I gave him a puzzled look. "That means my beloved."

"I like your choice in words, but I can tell this is going to be a difficult language to master."

"Don't worry, I'm a great teacher." He kissed my hand and asked, "What did you think of my *sza zad,* my squadron?"

I rubbed his hand against my cheek and pulled him closer. "I've always been a sucker for a man in uniform. Should I be saluting you?"

He chuckled. "No. You might be inclined to, though, if you'll allow me *udvarolni vkinek.* Let me translate." While his fingertips tickled me lightly on my midriff, he made a path of kisses up my neck. His tongue followed the trail back down and outward around my shoulders. Then he whispered in my ear as I was trying to pace my breaths, "Let me make love to you tonight."

"I don't want to get hurt."

He pulled back, held my face in his hands, looked into my eyes, and released a tiny teardrop of sincerity. "Don't you know by now that I would never do anything to hurt you?"

"Yes. But even though you want a divorce, you are still married."

"I told Elaine how I feel. That's why she's away this weekend. As soon as she gets back, we're going to put the house up for sale. Since I don't have the twenty grand to buy her out, she refuses to separate until it's sold."

His hands outlined the curve of my hips, and my fingers penetrated his mouth slowly, one at a time. I longed for him to devour every part of me. The silky brush of his chest hair tingled my satin nipples to an erection. As every nerve inside of me came alive, I welcomed him in a shuddering sensation. In afterglow, I tried to conceal my teardrops, which fell like dewdrops from a rose petal. I couldn't tell him that his silhouette in the moonlight was the thorn prickling me and that Evan's face was all I could see.

The next several months seemed like an eternity. He occasionally stopped by on Tuesday nights after his squadron meeting or on the way home from a search-and-rescue mission. Whenever he did come over, it was only to steal a few moments together. He tried to call me at least once on the weekends just to keep my hope alive. We went for eight months and had sex only twice. I wasn't happy about it. But I suppose I would've felt worse if he had come over, done his business and then left abruptly. I became one of the few who dreaded Friday afternoons at work, and I couldn't wait for Monday morning to come. Even when they couldn't get the asking price on their house and Elaine resorted to moving into an efficiency, he still refused to take chances in doing what normal lovers do: *date*. My patience was wearing thin, and I was at a breaking point when fate beat me to it.

It was late on a Sunday afternoon when I received his weekend call. I sensed that something was off, but he refused to talk about it over the phone. He asked me to meet him at a nearby marina. As I drove into the parking lot, my limbs became heavy and my insides tightened. My body never lied. My intuition was telling me to prepare for the bomb. He was standing at the edge of the dock, staring aimlessly out at the water. As I approached him, he turned around to face me. I put my arms around his neck, and he kissed me. Then he pulled my hands down and held them gently in his. I smelled beer on his breath, and I knew that I was in serious trouble since he rarely drank alcoholic beverages. His eyes were glazed red, and his eyelids were puffy. It looked like he had been crying.

He looked me directly in the eyes and said, "Honey, I'm sorry. We can't be together anymore."

"Why not?"

"Elaine's pregnant."

I immediately pulled my hands away. "What? You said you weren't sleeping with her anymore."

"I haven't been."

"Then how the hell did this happen?" I asked.

"Probably last month. I've been trying to fend off her advances to reconcile for months. She wouldn't take no for an answer, and I wanted to make sure that I didn't have feelings for her anymore."

I turned my back to him, looked drearily out at the water and wished that I had the courage to fall in and let myself be carried away by its swift current. "Then you still love her."

"No I don't. I love you. Do you think I would've put all of us through this aggravation by lying to both of you?"

I sighed deeply. "I don't know what to think anymore."

"Maybe this is better. You can go on your way and

be with someone like yourself who's never been married."

"How do you know this isn't just a ploy to get you to stay with her?" I asked.

"I don't. She has a doctor's appointment on Tuesday."

"So that's it. You're not even waiting until then before you break my heart." My throat painfully tightened, making my next breath an effort. And the tears came down, one after the other.

"I never intended to. Please believe me. I love you, but I have to do right by my child."

Following a long sob, I inhaled deeply. "If you loved me, you would be with me right now. You would've gotten a divorce months ago instead of dragging your feet. That would've been the *right* thing to do instead of sitting on the fence." He was silent. A burning sensation overcame me as though I was in the midst of a fireball. I didn't know which direction to take next, petrified of what was waiting for me around the corner. "How in the world am I supposed to go on? We work in the same building. How am I going to be able to stand seeing you every day?" My words made me aware of the painful road that I was headed down. He tried to hug me, but I pushed him away.

"I don't know."

"So she's moving back in the house?"

"She moved back in yesterday." He pleaded, with tears sliding down his unshaven face, "Please don't hate me." My tongue was twisted. I walked away without uttering another word or looking back at my soldier boy.

That night I didn't get any sleep. I wrestled with the memories and my actions since getting involved with him. His controlling mist had fallen over me, and his double standards and my resentment reigned. All the while, I hadn't even been having a real relationship with him. I had opportunities to date other men who were *available*. Both were attractive, responsible men who worked for IBM. I dated them briefly. When I didn't allow sexual or emotional intimacies to materialize, I quickly sabotaged any chance that I might've had with them. I was already acting like a submissive wife, feeling as though if I had any kind of a relationship with anyone else I would be cheating on him. My main agenda—besides to curb my loneliness—was to evoke jealousy within him. I got what I wanted, but more than I bargained for. I had previously taken some acting workshops and was getting called to go on auditions. He did not approve, and although he wasn't forcing me to give it up, I felt compelled to do so. Instead of using my leisure time to do the things I enjoyed, I worked hard to distract myself, cleaning homes and office buildings on the weekends.

I felt that I wasn't attentive enough toward Evan's needs. I lacked the maturity, insight, and experience to interpret his feelings. Thus, I overcompensated with Arthur. I pushed my needs and wants aside—not just because I wanted to be loved again—but because in some way that I wasn't even aware of, I was holding myself accountable for Evan's suicide. The ways in which I deprived myself weren't equitable retribution for the guilt I felt in being alive. Consciously, I was aware I had suffered a devastating blow. Subconsciously, I didn't know how deep the flesh wound was. I only knew that I never wanted to feel that kind of agony again. And one way to prevent it—I thought—was to become overly sensitive to everyone else's needs. By the time I was done building the barricade around myself, my needs and wants were shrouded in proving myself worthy to others, personally and professionally.

On the other hand, now the blisters of betrayal were rubbing my already bruised soul the wrong way and I couldn't run fast enough to get away from our manic affair. One week I was flying high with hope and could see a future with him. The next week I saw nothing but a hopeless and lonely road ahead. Yet if I had had an inkling of what the future with him was going to entail, I wouldn't have gotten on the seesaw to begin with. As an adult, I was making a concerted effort not to take on any of Helen's unfavorable traits. But when I fell under Arthur's charismatic spell and then became a woman scorned, I believe that I was tiptoeing into her terrain because I contemplated blowing his "faithful husband" cover to Elaine.

Instead, over the next month I went through several shades of sadness and depression. In the meantime, I worked hard to look for another job. We avoided each other as much as possible. Weeks later, I gave my notice and was leaving IBM. I secured a position at a local government engineering division. I was taking a cut in pay, but their benefits package would more than make up for it in the long run.

On my last day at IBM, some of my coworkers took me out to a farewell lunch. When I noticed that he wasn't joining us, I was relieved. Then shortly after I returned back to the site, I was called into the design and engineering office. As I opened the door, they all yelled, "Surprise!" When I saw streamers, balloons, and a cake, I got choked up. I cut the cake, and Arthur disappeared. But when I returned to my computer station, he was there waiting for me. When I saw him, I turned around and headed back down the hallway.

81

"Don't go," he said. "I have a surprise for you."

"Don't start with me. The last time you surprised me they almost had to assign me to an institution."

He clicked his tongue on the roof of his mouth. "Come on now. Don't be unreasonable."

"Don't treat me like a two-year-old. You're not my father."

"Elaine's gone back to New York. We got a contract on the house."

"When have I heard that before?" I was growing agitated. "I don't believe you anymore. You'll say anything just to get me back where you want me. You just want to gloat one last time over my pain. After today, I don't ever want to see you again."

"Don't say that," he said.

"I mean it. Don't bother calling because I'm changing my number to a private one."

"Okay." He walked out on the brink of tears.

About an hour later, our boss called me into his office to sign my exit interview papers. When we finished, he said, "I know it's none of my business. But speaking from experience, a married man doesn't turn his world upside down for another woman unless his intentions are serious. I know he's let you down before, but this time is different. Elaine left and is filing for divorce."

"Too little, too late," I said smugly.

"You're entitled to your feelings."

"Thank you." I gave him my badge and walked out the door with my pride intact, and with the sadness of saying good-bye and having another chapter of my life come to a close.

When I was walking out to my car, Arthur came up from behind. He grabbed my arm. "Please listen to me. Don't I deserve another chance?"

I pulled my arm away. "You had your chance, and you blew it. You ripped my heart out."

"Can't we just forget about the past and move on? There's nothing to stand in our way now."

I could tell by the paleness coloring his face that he felt exactly the way I felt several weeks before when he told me that it was over for good. I started walking faster, trying to make my escape before the salty waves that were cresting in my eyes splashed down my face. I didn't make it ten yards when I heard him shout, "I love you, and I don't want to live without you!" At once, I was back in time ignoring those silent pleas as Evan held me tightly.

I turned around and ran toward him. He swept me up into a strong embrace. I said, "I don't want to live without you either."

9

One hundred guests came to celebrate the union of the prince and princess in what was similar to the storybook wedding I had always dreamed of having. The ceremony was held at St. John's Catholic Church in North Side, a small town within Pittsburgh where the Ohio, Monongahela, and Allegheny Rivers converge. I walked up the white aisle canvas and followed the path of daisies that the flower girl had strewn at every other aisle post. The afternoon sun hit the stained-glass windows, shading the marble crucifix hanging behind the altar with violet-red and dark-blue tints. As I made my way past the glossy pine pews, the whispers of admiration made me glisten inside.

The floor-length, dove-white satin skirt contoured my figure sleekly. The satin bodice tapered my breasts in a sweetheart arc. The chiffon neckline and short cream-puff sleeves were sprinkled with pearl beads, and a Queen Anne collar wrapped an elegant satin choker around my neck.

I tried to remain focused on the savior in front of me. But my eyes shifted to Arthur, who was wearing a white linen tuxedo with a coattail jacket. His complete white ensemble set him apart from the ushers, whose cranberry ascot ties and cummerbunds accented their white tuxedos. I felt myself being pulled into a new and wondrous world, where European culture and family tradition blend. As I held the bouquet of white roses in front of me, I was praying that my nervousness wouldn't cause an embarrassing stumble. I briefly looked over at his mother, Ilona, who was sitting in the second row of pews. She was glowing with adulation at her handsome son. A wave of relief washed over me when I passed his father, Andras. He nodded in approval, then looked proudly on at his son, who was standing beside his cousin, Paul. Once the rings were presented, I removed my elbow-length glove, and the sparkling diamond band slid effortlessly on. Then I placed an identical band on my new husband's finger. Following the flickering candles' unison, Father Michael blessed the Eucharist offerings of bread and wine. Then everyone received Communion.

When all the guests returned quietly to their pews, Father Michael gestured for all to rise from their kneeling position. He announced, "You are now husband and wife according to the witness of the Holy Catholic Church and the laws of the state. Become one. Fulfill your promises. Love and serve the Lord. What God has united, man must not divide. Friends, I present to you for the first time, Mr. and Mrs. Concha." The sheer, chiffon veil of pearl beads was lifted, and our lips intermingled. The long train on the cathedral veil flowed behind as the ushers folded the aisle canvas in accordion pleats at the steps of the chancel.

An assortment of evergreen and pine trees guided the trail of white stretch limousines down Allegheny River Boulevard. Redbuds fringed the woodlands along the riverbank with deep-pink petals and purple threads of wisteria embroidered their way into the rolling hills of green tapestry. As the currents echoed underneath the brush of magnolia trees beside the Allegheny River, the daffodils were prancing to their spring march. As we traveled along the outskirts of Pittsburgh and deep into Penn Hills, we passed several golf courses. The day that I had been dreaming about most of my life continued at Hill Creek Resort.

While the guests sampled the hors d'oeuvres and wet their palettes with cocktails from the bar, the family and wedding party were posing for pictures. Once we finished eating dinner almost two hours later, Arthur and I danced underneath the crystalline chandeliers and on the marble ballroom floor to "Lady in Red." Andras came to cut in. His request was in his mother tongue: *"Tancra felkerni?"*

Throughout the last several months, I learned to use one Hungarian phrase very well. *"Nem ertem."* (I don't understand.)

Andras repeated the question in English. "May I dance with my son's beautiful bride?" I pulled up my satin teal bridesmaid dress slightly and curtsied. Arthur dispersed into the crowd and made his way over to a small fountain that was brimming with champagne. Moments later, he offered a toast as the best man.

As reality would have it, I was not the princess, nor was Arthur the prince captured in the spotlight. We weren't lost in the rapture of the wedding song. The couple on the four-tier wedding cake, which was decorated with teal and cranberry rosettes, didn't portray either of us. Nor were we the playful couple feeding each other wedding cake in the corner of the country club ballroom. Our names didn't grace the cocktail napkins. And as everyone toasted the union, our wedding date wasn't etched into the crystal goblets. Rather, it was Paul and his college sweetheart, Sonya, who had vowed to love each other for life. And it was their wedding—not mine—that brought me hundreds of miles to meet my husband's family, in their entirety, for the first time.

While Paul and Sonya opened their wedding gifts, some of Arthur's relatives were sitting down for a few quiet family moments. His sister, Faye, was admiring my engagement ring. "Wow! I never knew my brother was such a big spender. It's beautiful."

"Thank you. I get a lot of compliments on it." The sad truth was that not only did I get cheated out of a wedding, but we didn't even have wedding bands when we got married, let alone an engagement ring. I bought Arthur's excuse that money was tight, being new homeowners and all. So wedding bands were a luxury. Yet to him, spending five hundred dollars on a new set of sport radial tires for his truck, just two weeks later, was a necessity. It took me almost three months of nagging to get him to break down and buy the cheapest set of gold bands. As far as my *worse* half was concerned, I wasn't worthy of a diamond. And the cubic zirconia that I was parading, which he tried to pawn off on me months after we were married as the real thing, was a dreadful presage of the value he placed on me.

"Arthur, I noticed that you didn't accept Communion. Been a bad boy lately?" Robert, Arthur's brother, teased.

Andras kidded him further, directing his attention toward me. "Arthur has always been the lost sheep. Even as a child, whatever we forbid him to do, he usually did it anyway. Right, son?" His accent was thick. It was impossible for him to conceal his past and that he had spent the first half of his life in another country.

"I rebelled just to spite you, right Mummy?" Ilona grinned but studied hard to watch the expressions of the others as they engaged in conversation. After spending the past two days with her, I recognized her bewildering smile. I could tell that she could not completely comprehend what was being said. She was relying on her ability to decipher the art of expression, mimicking what the others around her were doing to compensate for the language barrier. Arthur mocked her in her expressions by smiling and nodding silently. The conversation was in English for my benefit and Faye's fiancé, John. Otherwise, when they were among themselves, they spoke in Hungarian.

After Arthur translated, Ilona said, "Arthur has hard head."

Robert wasn't going to let this go. "So bro', I guess that means that you haven't been to confession lately either."

"Drop it, shithead," Arthur warned.

Faye, who was following in her mother's religious footsteps, asked, "You still go to Mass, don't you?"

"What is this?—an inquisition." Arthur asked. He looked over at Ilona, knowing that she understood the question. "We try to attend Mass every week."

"Did you get your first marriage annulled?" Faye asked.

"Not yet," Arthur answered.

Robert tipped his champagne goblet on its crystal base, and his fingers circled the top of it. "I was beginning to think that since Shoshanah's a Hebrew name, she's Jewish, and you've secretly converted."

Arthur replied, "You know what they say when you assume anything."

Robert looked at me. "Then you must be Catholic because you didn't seem to have a problem reciting most of the words."

"Wrong again," I said, biting my top lip.

When it came to matters of religion, Ilona was

quick. She asked, "Your family Christian?"

"I'm sorry," I said. "I don't mean to sound rude, but it's against my religion to discuss my faith." Silence overcame the table momentarily. I had never stepped a foot inside a church until I got married. I felt like a lost sheep, attending because I wanted God to be in our marriage and I wanted to become acquainted with Catholicism. This was in large part so that the family that I hoped to create with Arthur would be united in one faith.

Arthur and I never accepted Communion, and I always wanted us to make our exit at that point in the service. But he thought it was rude to leave before the final hymn was over. So we sat in silent observation. I wondered what was behind the stares of members of the congregation as they stood patiently with their hands clasped together in front of them during the procession. When they passed us by, gave us the once-over, and probably mentally questioned which of the Ten Commandments we had broken, I always felt unworthy. I started associating guilt as being the universal platform that's paramount in all organized religion. It reminded me of what went on in the congregation that I was forced to be a member of growing up. The same nonsense that now, as an adult, I was made to feel like a stranger in my own family. This was due to the battle lines that had been drawn between those who followed the doctrines of the Jehovah's Witnesses and those who didn't. According to Father, there were no gray areas when it came to religion. One was either a baptized Witness or a wicked worshiper of the devil. It was his way or no way. Even though I had been separated from him and the organization for several years, the effects were still manifesting themselves and difficult to disguise.

One distinguishing feature that I saw in Catholicism, which I admired, was that they didn't hold public ostracizing ceremonies and crucify individuals who had sinned in front of the entire congregation. Nor did they disown their own on the basis of pious reasoning and religious incongruity. It was a struggle on a daily basis to eradicate the beliefs that the cult had brainwashed me with. Thus, I was in an underlying constant search to replace their false truths with those of a more spiritual nature, a faith where I felt comfortable and complete in its philosophy.

"Shoshanah, your family in Florida?" Ilona asked.

"Yes." The second subject that I wanted to avoid and was most ashamed of was my severely dysfunctional family. But I knew that it would be impossible to make it through this family reunion without some reference to my beginnings.

"You see them?" Ilona persisted.

"After my mother died when I was very young, my father remarried. He's busy with his second family and running a business." I was still using Helen as Father's scapegoat. I couldn't admit to myself that he just didn't give a damn about me, plain and simple—and that was the real reason he wasn't in my life—not because he was a religious fanatic.

In dialect she could comprehend, Arthur gave her a succinct version. I knew the question was bound to come up, so I had briefed him earlier about what to say when it did. He was to explain that I considered myself better off if I kept distance between myself and some members of my family. I didn't want him to go into the details of the backward religion that I was raised in or the family who lacked university educations, especially since I knew how much value his family placed on those issues. If I thought I could have gotten away with it, I would have said I was an orphan, which wouldn't have been stretching the truth by much.

Although his family welcomed me with open arms once they became better acquainted with who I was, they intimidated me. They weren't wealthy socialites who indulged in pretentious pursuits to showcase their status. But their European, aristocratic background demanded nothing less than purebred intellects, an area where Arthur was constantly made to feel as though he didn't measure up. They had more respect for someone with a doctorate degree who was destitute than they had for a self-made millionaire who lacked a formal education but became successful in America's free enterprise system.

Andras came to my rescue. "Well one thing I want to know is how such an ugly mutt like Arthur got such a beautiful and sweet girl to be his wife."

"Oh you haven't heard," I said. "I'm almost legally blind."

Andras laughed along with all the others. "And she even has a sense of humor."

"I'm glad you approve, sir," I said. "One of my major character flaws is that I hate to disappoint others."

"Now that you've mentioned disappointments," Robert said in a haughty manner. "Arthur, have you gone on any missions lately with your toy soldiers?"

"A few . . . and for your information, I'm only a couple of exams away from making captain's status."

"Very good," Andras affirmed.

Robert asked, "Does that mean you'll be eligible to fly if they need you?" Before Arthur could answer, he continued, "I almost forgot about that weak stomach of yours grounding you."

This hit Arthur below the belt. He didn't like college, and he found studying difficult. The only reason he went to college was because his parents pressured him into doing so. The Officer's Training Program at the Naval Academy only accepted applicants with nothing less than a bachelor's degree. After he earned his degree, he had the ambition to become a top-gun navy pilot. Elaine, his girlfriend at the time, couldn't endure the separation. He had allowed his airborne dream to crash and burn so that he wouldn't lose her. This is the story that he told me during my infatuation stage with him. He said, "That reminds me, fart face, how'd you escape that eating disorder clinic? Either you're having a relapse of anorexia, or maybe it's AIDS."

"It would be tragic," Faye said. "But it wouldn't surprise me . . . with all the women that he's had."

Andras looked at John. "See what you have to look forward to when you join our family?"

This kind of bantering went on throughout the rest of the reception. Even though I knew there was no malicious intent behind it, I began to recognize the foundation that created the less than desirable side of Arthur's character. Demeaning each other was their sport.

As the two doves that were kept in a cage at the entrance to the ballroom were set free, the blissful newlyweds drove off into the sunset. The rest of the family went back to my in-laws' house.

Their house was a split-level ranch. The brick exterior kept the interior well insulated, obstructing the harsh snow drifts of late fall and winter. It sat at the top of a hill, along with a dozen other homes. At night, the spectacular city lights lit up the valley below. As old man winter appeared, the summer meadows transformed into giant snow cones with translucent ice crystals at the peak of the Allegheny Mountains.

I respected my in-laws for many reasons, but the most outstanding one was for the several sacrifices they made to make their children's future better than the generations that preceded them. This was unlike my family dynamic, where Father and Helen lived by the motto "children last."

Regardless of the weather or his limited leisure time on weekends, Andras took his sons to Little League practice, Boy Scouts, and other activities that were offered by the YMCA. To cut down on household expenses and save for their children's education, they got by on one automobile. This posed a problem when the boys were in high school and wanted to date. Ilona and Andras didn't socialize much, primarily because they couldn't afford it while the children were growing up. And Ilona didn't want to leave her children alone with strangers. By the time their sons entered high school, they were already accustomed to spending most Saturday evenings at home with their family. So it wasn't a large sacrifice to them if one of them wanted to use the car for a Saturday night date.

Robert loved school and got rewarded for his good grades by being allowed to use the car to go out on weekends. On the other hand, Arthur loathed school, doing the bare minimum to graduate. His punishment for poor grades was not being allowed to use the car. As a result, he didn't date much. Most of his weekends were spent helping Andras with chores around the house and yard. He was more content working with his hands than he was mastering his mind inside schoolbooks. He didn't suffer from the effects of this choice until he was a junior in high school. His low SAT scores forced him to spend the two years following his high school graduation inside a community college—unlike Robert and Faye. They made their second homes inside a dormitory.

Ilona was no different from most housewives of her generation. Her whole world revolved around taking care of her family. She and Andras were strict parents, enforcing curfews and moral codes. According to Arthur, affection wasn't displayed casually, nor were feelings discussed often. Nonetheless, he experienced a strong dose of love through their moral and financial support.

The difference in how Arthur and I were raised was extreme. He learned to trust at an early age. He knew that no matter what he did, his parents might not agree with him, but they would accept him. When people I had to depend on for my survival became the executioners of my childhood innocence, I learned not to trust. His parents were generous and selfless. Mine made daily withdrawals from my self-esteem bank, and I was stuck spending the rest of my life paying off their insidious debt. The only parallel in our childhoods was that we were both raised in a religious environment. Ilona shouldered most of that responsibility though, with Andras attending Mass only on holidays. The acceptance from his parents was as necessary to him as oxygen was to his lungs. After I met them and saw the hold that they had over him, I understood why he was so insistent that we marry only six months after his and Elaine's divorce became final.

The rest of the family stayed upstairs talking while Ilona and I went downstairs to the basement. She showed me family photo albums. Perhaps she was testing the soil or planting the seeds. I was just happy that I had finally found a garden where I could grow. Her kind spirit watered my thirsty soul. I felt as though she was looking through the tiny keyhole into my tower of seclusion. It was like she knew exactly how to unlock the door to my heart and aid in the reparation process. When she tucked me into bed, I touched her lightly on the cheek. As she kissed me good night, a vine of love started to grow along the wall that I had erected, and the receding petals of the forsaken flower began to open.

Arthur's cold feet awakened me from my peacefulness. "Aren't you glad that we didn't have a wedding?" he asked. "You see the way my parents acted at the reception. They were like wallflowers and weren't very friendly to Sonya's family. I can only imagine what they would do if they met your family."

"They may surprise you."

"Don't get your hopes up, honey. Be thankful that there was no big hoopla when we got married. I saved you from severe disappointment."

"Like the way that you saved me from disappointment when you passed off a cubic zirconia as a diamond. "

"I've had to endure the last couple of days listening to my parents brag about Robert. I must have heard about every accomplishment he has ever made and where his wonderful life is headed. Drop it! Having a nice house is more important than a stupid ring or big wedding. It's only for show anyway."

My biggest letdown and thief was laying beside me, stealing whatever comforting covers I had left to hide under and indulge in my storybook fantasies. Having to sleep with the big bad wolf was a small price to pay to a little girl who got to visit a safe place a couple of times a year. Going to see the family who was willing to give me a chance also gave me a true sense of belonging. I tried to retreat back into the peaceful calm that Ilona had left me in and fight off the memories of my own wedding night. It was my wedding night when I pulled back the covers and discovered a poisonous toad, the one who had been hiding underneath his sheets of deception.

I skipped along the yellow brick road with rose-colored glasses. I was taken to a land where storybook legends struggle to stay alive. I refused to let this relationship, along with an opportunity to have some sense of normalcy in my life, die in long suffering.

10

During our brief courtship, I had found a place in Arthur's arms where I wanted to stay. Though we had talked about marriage, I was hoping for a long engagement. I had no reservations about making a commitment not to forsake him for another, and I was certain that I could keep that promise even if we didn't tie the knot. The institution of marriage frightened me. I thought that as soon as I signed a piece of paper that declared my sin of falling in love with a married man, my dreams would go up in a puff of smoke. Arthur, on the other hand, wanted something more concrete. He wanted a legally binding contract, uniting us and our bank accounts. For fear of losing the man I loved, I pushed my feelings aside and tried to fulfill his every desire.

Even though we were only living together, I exhausted all of my funds to help clean up the financial residue that his previous marriage left behind. A wish that I willingly granted him was to help replace the house he lost in his divorce. Cashing in my certificates of deposit and all but depleting my savings account was a tiny sacrifice. In exchange, I figured I had reserved a bottomless well of gratitude where he was concerned. When I realized that his income was just as necessary to my survival in the current circumstances as mine was, the walls started to close in. I was haunted by the feelings of being a helpless child forced to live under Father's tyrannical reign and experiencing Jim's manipulation tactics and blackmail. Despite my efforts to suppress it, the fear of being trapped where someone else has control over my life filtered in. The religious belief, of the man being the head of his household and his wife becomes his submissive servant, lingered.

My youthful resilience and aspirations took over. I blindly trusted in love, having faith that when I jumped into the water, my lessons from the past would keep me afloat. I would never be at anyone's mercy again. Arthur reassured me that over time we would recoup my investment. So I pushed my reservations aside, and we purchased a home together. Six months later, I felt that the next logical step was to give in to his marriage proposal.

Although we had a civil ceremony, we mutually agreed to postpone having a formal wedding and honeymoon for a year. This afforded him the time to get his first marriage annulled as well as keeping ours quiet. His brother and a couple of work associates were the only ones he told. By the time he got around to telling the rest of his family and friends, we had already been married a few months. His rationale was that he was protecting me from the unfavorable reception, which he guaranteed I would receive, if the dirty secret were exposed too soon. The waiting period would give his parents time to digest the reality that I was his new wife instead of the mistress of mystery that he had hidden away. So in a sense, he was still treating me like his mistress, even after we had lived together six months before getting married. The truth was that he felt embarrassed for jumping into a second marriage so soon. It took me months to come out of denial and face how this made me feel. I wasn't worthy enough to be introduced to his family or friends as his wife. I was to be hidden away in some closet as if I was a dirty basket of laundry that needed to be bleached white. Yet even more disturbing than this was the side of himself that he revealed to me on our wedding night.

When we finished exchanging vows inside the colorless chambers of the courthouse, we celebrated over dinner at a restaurant. We arrived home an hour later, where I was planning a night to remember. Within minutes, the telephone rang. Though I pleaded with him not to answer the call, when he recognized the voice on the answering machine as being one of his peers from his squadron group, he did anyway.

I tried not to let my annoyance with him ruin my sensual mood. I figured that the few minutes that he would be engaged in conversation would give me the time I needed to transpose myself into a love goddess. I changed into sexy lingerie, which I concealed under a plain bathrobe. After waiting forty-five minutes for him to end the conversation, my erotic mood diminished. I sat down next to him on the sofa and tried to give him a silent signal. Once I realized that he had finished discussing business and was just blowing the breeze, I was sensing the subtle change in him. He was settling into his comfort zone, and I was being taken for granted.

As I sat brooding over my second-class citizenship, the feelings from childhood (of being neglected) instantly resurfaced. I deduced that he obviously placed greater value on his rank inside his squadron than he did on my feelings or desires. It was a stage where he could showcase his aspirations, and it would make up for the disappointment he caused Andras when he was honorably discharged from the Naval Academy. Similarly, Father held on tightly to the religious reins that empowered him, forfeiting a relationship with myself and most of my siblings. Blood, and anyone who didn't worship him, was only dead weight resting on his throne. Both men were suffering from the same inconsiderate syndrome.

By the time Arthur finished his conversation, I was in the guestroom, laying on the bed and sulking. He came in and asked, "What's wrong?"

"You mean you actually don't know?"

He quickly became annoyed. "No. I can't read your mind."

"I accepted having to postpone a traditional wedding and honeymoon and the fact that I'm spending my wedding night at home. But I won't just lie down and take this."

"Take what?" he asked.

"You're ignoring me on a night that can't be replaced. At least for once in my life, I should be able to feel like I'm someone special. When you picked up the phone, you slapped me in the face."

"Wait a minute. You knew that I had to help Ronnie with the banquet tomorrow night. We were discussing last-minute details."

"Fine, but why did you stay on the phone for forty-five minutes?"

"Quit exaggerating. I wasn't on the phone for forty-five minutes."

"Yes you were. Look at the clock. Bullshitting on the phone is obviously more important to you than spending time with your wife on your wedding night." As soon as I spoke those words, I caught a glimpse of my future, a future with a man whom I was now bound to by marital vows and had just signed over my life to. I wondered, if he cares so little about my

100

feelings just hours after we're married, what is he going to be like in the days to come?

I struck a nerve, and he blew. "Why do women have to blow this marriage thing way out of proportion? All you women do is dress yourselves up in fairy tales. This is real life! Did you ever stop to consider what I wanted?"

"You got what you wanted!" I screamed. Every penny I earned and saved is sitting right here in this house! If you had no intentions of taking the marriage vow to honor me seriously, why did you insist on marrying me?"

"If we didn't get married by the end of this month, IRS would've slaughtered me in taxes this year."

"What are you talking about?" I asked.

"I swear, for the smart woman that I thought you were when I met you, you are turning out to be incredibly stupid. Between the salary I made this past year and being able to claim only a few months of mortgage interest, if I file under single status, I will owe them thousands. I lost a lot because you wanted me to get a divorce. I'm not going to give away another penny that I don't have to." Without my even realizing it then, he was injecting me with a heavy dose of guilt.

"I didn't want this house! What do we need with three bedrooms? A villa would've been enough."

"Quit talking like you have a paper asshole! You don't know anything about real estate. I've bought and sold two homes."

"I see now," I said. "Everything for you, and nothing for me! Don't you think I deserve to feel special on my wedding night?" My eyes were wet with tears.

His teeth gnashed together with every brutal

101

word. "What makes you think you deserve anything special? You're not special, so quit acting like a spoiled princess! You're lower than a piece of shit!"

Shock overcame me. No one had ever said those demeaning words to me—not Father or Jim. Those deflowering words damaged me more than anything I could've ever imagined. Having my possessions destroyed or the biting sting of a belt didn't erode my soul as quickly as those words did. I had seen a selfish side to him before. But during the time that we had been living together, regardless of whatever stress was upon us, he never called me names. The blow came out of nowhere and was so intense that it left my shell standing where he had struck me. From that point forward, I walked outside of it.

As he drove away in an angry rage, I felt the prison bars close in on me, and the cell of insanity crept in. This time it wasn't my age that kept me in bondage, as it had when I was a child, where I was forced to remain under Father's roof until I was old enough to legally flee. Rather, it was foolishness on my part for trusting a man who picked his wedding night to lay down his law. My initial reaction was to pack a duffel bag and leave, but then I realized that I didn't have enough funds to start over in a place of my own again.

I was dangling from a cloud of indecision, and I attributed this vacillation to the belief that I finally got what I deserved. God finally answered my prayers by giving me what I wanted. I equated all the panic I was experiencing as possible self-sabotage on my part. This cognitive fog ended up immobilizing me to the point where I couldn't make the decision to stay or leave. The scales of truth were offset by the anxiety of having to flee my home and be alone once again. The cost of freedom wasn't nearly as distressing as my plight to hang on to the love that I thought I had shared with him in the beginning of our relationship. I took to heart what he had said about my playing up the fantasy in my head of what my wedding day should have been like. I imagined it would be a day when a woman is transformed into a princess and her husband into a prince. There they express their everlasting love and devotion to each other. From that time, the two build a kingdom of happiness. Together their love forms a bridge that connects their hearts forever. No matter what befalls them, they'll always have, share, and protect that sacred and safe place. But unfortunately in my fairy tale, there was a monster stalking me in the moon shadow and chasing me across the bridge back to my dark past.

My entire childhood was centered on what other people were feeling and how I was to appease them. Instead of feeling like a member in a family unit, I felt like just another brick in Father's pyramid of power. His voice and Helen's were the only ones spoken. If I was caught expressing my opinion, especially if it was to disagree, the consequence was heavy. A facial expression, sigh, or whimper was a sign of disobedience, resulting in punishment. Whatever feelings I developed I had to hide. Before long, I had difficulty identifying with my feelings or forming my own identity. This pattern set a detrimental precedent as I got older.

It was after losing Evan that my inner strength was tested, and I began to evolve. I stood up to the challenge by continuing to move forward, improve myself, and make my life better. While on my road to recovery, I took a detour into a dark tunnel before a total emergence was complete. No, I couldn't blame Father, Helen, or my backward religious upbringing for my current predicament. I could only hold myself accountable for the choice I made. The same choice that forced me into a psychiatrist's office on a late Sunday afternoon when Arthur told me that he and Elaine had reconciled. I continued my counseling sessions and my medical treatment preceding his divorce. Soon after, I terminated my sessions and flushed the antidepressants down the toilet, thinking that the only cure to what ailed me was our being together.

Within a couple of hours, Arthur returned home. His temper cooled, and he started to cry. "I'm so sorry. Please forgive me. I didn't mean what I said. I've been under a lot of stress at work."

"What do you mean?"

"I didn't want to worry you, but there's talk about layoffs again. I just don't know what I'm going to do if I lose my job. I'm so specialized in what I do. I'll never make that kind of money again. Don't you think I feel awful that I can't give you a nice wedding right now or take you on a honeymoon? I feel like a failure."

My tears melted into his as I reassured him. "You're not a failure. Don't worry. If you lose your job, you'll find something else. We'll make it somehow."

While he carried me off to bed to consummate our marriage, I brushed aside my instincts to flee. Maybe I was being too hard on him, I reasoned. I owed it to the both of us to give the marriage an honest effort.

His suspicions were accurate: Contracts were being cut drastically, and IBM was downsizing. As Friday mornings approached, he was on pins and needles, hoping that a pink slip wasn't in his paycheck. While he managed to escape the first round of cutbacks, he wasn't as lucky on the second. When his contract company lost the bidding war, no one was exempt from losing their position. After he lost his job, he looked through the classified ads and contacted every headhunter nationwide for the next three months. He was hanging on to the hope that the contract company, which had won the bid for IBM, was going to recruit him, as it had already started hiring some of his previous coworkers. The only offers he received were out of state. If he took any of these, it would mean that we would be separated for months. And if our budget allowed, we would reunite one weekend a month. The pay scales had dropped because of all the technical schools (like mine) that were popping up everywhere. Therefore, the offers that were coming in weren't substantial enough to offset paying a rent and landscape maintenance on our yard. So the extra money that we had managed to save since purchasing our home was disappearing fast. He tried to quiet my anxiety over the financial duress we were under by reassuring me that his parents would help us out. Of course, coming from the background that I did, it was like he was speaking to me in a foreign language. The idea that we could look to his parents for assistance wasn't something that I had ever experienced.

Professionally speaking, things weren't much better for me. Though South Florida was growing rapidly, the effects of the recession were still lingering. And county government was reluctant to hire anyone new unless it was absolutely necessary. I had been hired as a drafting technician in a division whose responsibility it was to update the road map database for the county. A stack of changes came in on a weekly basis. My position had been vacant for eight months before I arrived, so I spent the first three months just trying to get the system up-to-date. I had passed my probation and was in my department for seven months when the next position above me became available. The position came not only with a status change but also with a considerable pay increase. After having been diligent in bringing the system up-to-date and already being in the department, I was certain that I had an outstanding chance of getting the promotion versus an outsider who wasn't familiar with their system. It was an unbelievable slap in the face when my boss hired a man who didn't even have a degree. When I approached my boss and asked him why he didn't choose me, I was told that the male whom he hired had a wife and child. I, on the other hand, was being partially supported by my husband. This infuriated me to no end. Within two months, I found another position, and my salary increased by fifty percent. As for the man who had been hired for the position that I wanted, well, he gave his notice the same week that I left.

Arthur eventually resigned himself to the fact that he wasn't going to get back into IBM. He decided to take a local government position for considerably less than what he had previously been earning. However, it was a permanent position that included great benefits. When he was hired as a draftsman and not as a designer, not only did he take a cut in pay, but he also took a step back professionally. This, and the fact that my salary was higher than his, was an enormous threat to his ego. He was no longer applauding my accomplishments but rather belittling my every endeavor.

His howl for control in every area of our household muffled any voice I had while I was falling into lust. Though I internally questioned some of his choices, I lacked the confidence and strength to speak my mind. When I stood by man's privilege to dictate, I lost true feminine consciousness. I threw caution to the wind and tried to focus on his worthy qualities.

Shortly, though, my worry over seeing more unfavorable traits in him surface every day carried me into a land of weary. I felt that I had no control over my body or mind. If I told anyone about the thoughts I had been having of impending doom and dreaded fear, which were accompanied by a rapid pulse, sweaty palms, and hyperventilating, they might lock me up and throw away the key. At least that's the way Arthur made me feel. According to him, if I went to any professionals who deal with diagnosing and treating anyone struggling with a mental illness, I had the psychotic plague. I was afraid of being stigmatized as a misfit, the way he made me feel when he witnessed one of these episodes.

I was trapped inside the car for forty-five minutes while Arthur launched his attack, berating me with the worst vulgar language that I had ever heard. I can't recall why he was mad at me. But I was beginning to understand that he didn't need a reason. His tirade stopped briefly as we pulled into the parking lot and went inside a mall to eat lunch.

As soon as we entered the food court area, it was as if my head had become a basketball court and the patrons were the fans shouting in the bleachers. My pulse dribbled from one end of a court of confusion to the other in madness. Suddenly, my ears echoed with every sound filling the entire area. My mind was overrun by every major event and every trivial detail of my life—and none of it made any sense. I found a vacant bench outside the dining area and laid down on it. He was embarrassed and reprimanded me. "What do you think you're doing? You're not a child! Now get up!"

"I can't."

He grabbed my arm. "Yes you can. Now sit up."

"My arms and legs are numb. I only feel sharp tingles in them." My heartbeat was echoing inside my ears. I placed two fingers on my neck. "My heart is racing. Oh God, what if I'm having a heart attack?"

"Get your head out of your ass and quit worrying about how you're fucking feeling," he said in a harsh but low manner. "You look ridiculous." When he noticed that I had broken out into a sweat, he took my pulse. "Just relax. You're only making it worse." He went to one of the vendors and brought back a small paper bag and some damp napkins. "Here. Breathe into the bag and wipe your face with these. You're probably just hyperventilating. Do you have any chest pains?"

"No."

"It's probably just your nerves. If you calm down, it will pass."

Twenty minutes later, when full sensation returned to my legs and arms, I managed to walk back to the car. Because I was still feeling like I had had an out-of-body experience, though I knew that I hadn't died, I insisted that he take me to the emergency room at the nearest hospital. The physician on call confirmed that I had had a panic attack. I was prescribed antianxiety medication and urged to practice relaxation techniques. When Arthur learned that I was in no physical danger, he became angry and blamed me for bringing the episode on myself.

Between performing my domestic duties and working full time, I couldn't afford the sluggish mode the medication put me into. And thinking that I had to rely on medication to control my thoughts and feelings made me feel as though I was a weakling. While I lacked self-assertiveness, I didn't want the medication to become a crutch or a means to mask the real issues, causing me to suppress my feelings further. Yet that's exactly what I was doing. My marriage vows were confining me into a forced institution, an asylum where I was searching for any escape before I lost myself completely.

When I suppressed these feelings further, they inevitably manifested into other parts of my body. The stress to financially keep everything going and keep him happy was wearing me down so badly that my appetite decreased immensely. Whenever I did eat a meal, within an hour I was in the bathroom watching the remains of it getting flushed down the toilet. The nausea induced me to vomit or my intestines tensed up, causing me to exhibit symptoms similar to that of a spastic colon. Hence, I became severely dehydrated. I felt as though something wasn't right in my body. This intuition sent me to a doctor, whom after performing an upper-and-lower GI series, found nothing out of the ordinary. The more I insisted that something was wrong with me, the more annoyed Arthur became, like the day a doctor finally took me seriously.

I woke one morning feeling incredibly weak. The lack of nutrients in my system made me lightheaded, and my vision was obscured periodically with black spots. I practically begged Arthur to stay home from work so that he could drive me to my doctor's appointment. He wasn't happy that I had ruffled his compassionless feathers. I put some clothes on and laid my head in his lap while he watched television. I was panting like a puppy, looking for any strokes of attention he was willing to give. His hands remained by his side. He ignored me as the morning talk show captivated him. Then I made a direct attempt to evoke sympathy from him by placing his hand on my head, thinking that he would get the message. He sighed heavily, and words of ice rolled from his tongue. "Put on some makeup. You look like you just stepped out of a morgue."

His thoughtless comment magnified my feeble state, and I interpreted his words of scorn. *You're not the love of my life or my angel.* I lacked the physical strength to get up and shake him to his senses. I wanted to ask where the charming man with whom I had shared lunch hours in the park had gone. Where did the innocent boy, who rested his eyes while I massaged his temples until he fell asleep in my lap, run off to? More so, I wanted to know how I could bring him back and what had I done to turn him into a heartless stranger.

When we got to the doctor's office and I stepped on the scale, someone finally took notice, recognizing that I had dropped ten pounds within a few weeks. Then, when the challenge to draw blood had become futile, I was immediately admitted into the hospital for de-hydration. I was fed intravenously to increase my electrolytes. After three days of running various tests on my digestive system and all the results came back normal, they concluded that psychological stress was the culprit.

Our cupboards of love remained bare for more than a year. I tried every recipe in the book, using the same ingredients of compassion, forgiveness, patience, and understanding each time. Yet whatever I tried con-tinued to fail, because I kept getting the same result. My hesitation to omit the grave ingredient that was choking my spirit and wanting to save face sent me into a nosedive. I continued to color my perception of abuse, thinking that just because I wasn't getting physically abused it was tolerable. The pebble and the stone had been cast, and the boulder was on its way.

11

The flaming fireball of dawn emerged from the ocean's horizon, blushing the skyline canvas with orange and pink hues. Plastic candy canes hung from the street lamps that bordered the parkways. Festival lights draped trees, homes, and buildings. As Arthur and I took a scenic route before arriving at the hospital, morning was breaking. Should I die on the operating table, I didn't want to miss another sunrise. With Christmas only a few weeks away, the only gift I wanted was to awaken from my surgery and have a second chance at life.

The vigil that I silently held the night before wasn't enough to quiet my worst fear. Nor did it anesthetize my feelings of regret for the dreams and desires that I failed to fulfill, the many places that I wanted to visit and hadn't, and the unresolved issues and questions that I needed answers to. Yet beyond all these was the person whom I had aspirations of becoming, the one who would perish the moment that I did.

"I just had my blood drawn two days ago. I won't have any left for the surgery," I complained to the male pre-op nurse as he tightened the tourniquet.

He noticed my damp skin and that I was trembling. He rubbed my hand before searching for a pronounced vein. "Sorry, honey, Dr. Epstien's orders. He wants to make sure your potassium level is normal. Otherwise, he's going to postpone surgery. Make a tight fist for me."

"I hope not. I drank an entire gallon of orange juice yesterday. I'm beginning to wonder if doctors don't have a contract with Dracula."

He chuckled. "I don't see any black capes or coffins lying around here. Do you?"

"No. But I don't want to wake up from my surgery inside a dark drawer."

"Don't complain," Arthur interrupted. "He's only doing his job. Besides, if you die, you won't know a thing. I'm the one who'll be stuck with all the debt."

The nurse bent down and mumbled sympathetically, "What a comforting husband you have. He's so uplifting." Then he flicked a vein a few times before lifting his head up. "Okay folks, I think we've got a winner . . . just a little stick." I turned my head away, unable to watch my blood filling the vial. He released the tourniquet. "You can open your hand now." He noticed that my breathing had become shallow. "Relax, and take a couple of deep breaths."

When I exhaled, it was along the lines of an anxious sigh. "Has Dr. Lucos ever lost a patient?" I asked.

"No. He's got one of the best track records here."

"There's always a first," Arthur said. When he saw a look of astonishment come over the nurse, he added, "Just kidding." Then he asked, "What about Dr. Epstien?"

"I've never seen him here before, so I don't know. What procedure are you having done?"

"As far as I know, a radical mastoidectomy," I said.

"According to the MRI, there's some kind of mass behind her left ear," Arthur added. "They think it's benign and probably just an infection. But they won't know for sure until they get inside."

"I almost don't care what they find as long as they can make this vertigo disappear," I said.

113

The nurse touched the side of my face, then said, "I've had that a couple of times when I had a bad ear infection. It's not pleasant. Anyway, you must be special because I rarely see a patient who gets to have two surgeons in the operating room at the same time."

"If you only knew," Arthur said.

"There—all done. See that wasn't so bad." He placed labels on the vials. Then he handed me a plastic cup to urinate in. "I need a sample before I can take these up to the lab."

Within two hours, I was staring up at spotlights. An oxygen mask was placed over my nose and mouth. Dr. Epstien rubbed my forehead. I looked at Dr. Lucos, who was the chief surgeon performing the surgery, with Dr. Epstien assisting. Dr. Lucos placed his hands inside a pair of surgical gloves. He smiled kindly, then he said, "Don't worry. Everything's going to be okay."

"Do you have any nice places you'd like to visit?" Dr. Epstien asked.

My eyes blinked heavily. "Yes, the Smoky Mountains."

"It's very pretty there, isn't it?" I watched Dr. Epstien nod to the anesthesiologist. "I want you to count backward from one hundred." As I passed the number ninety, I heard Dr. Lucos wish me pleasant dreams.

Four hours later, I was wheeled into the recovery room, where I fought to keep my eyes open long enough to concentrate on my surroundings. *I made it. I'm alive. Thank you, God.* The post-op nurse checked my vitals. As the blue-gray walls blended with the glossy floor and the scurry of nurses, my head was throbbing with pain and my vision was blurry. "Don't try to focus on anything. It will just make you dizzy and nauseous," she said. I tried moving my mouth to speak. But the excruciating pain turned my efforts into inaudible murmurs, followed by long moans. "Sorry, honey. I know you're in pain and thirsty. But we can't give you anything for another four hours."

As I was being wheeled to my room, I woke up only long enough to faintly make out Jay. He had a bunch of roses in his hand. "You made it, Peaches. You're okay."

The next time I briefly awoke I recognized the voice of Julia. "Don't fight it, honey. Go back to sleep. We'll be here."

While I drifted back to sleep, I heard a tone of exasperation attached to these words. "She's always so afraid she's going to die." *Ah, yes.* It was my *beloved* husband. His uncompassionate side was rearing its ugly head again, testing the milieu for any rebuttals. He exercised tremendous restraint, having to spend the entire day, and now night, trapped inside a hospital. I had lived with him long enough to know that if there were someway for him to avoid it, he would have rather spent the time somewhere else, far away from the grim reaper.

The rationale side of him was fighting with an ominous omen of guilt. He thought that he planted his seed of sin inside my soul when he committed adultery and broke his holy covenant with the Catholic Church. This guilt overshadowed any prayers he might have offered on my behalf, his partner in crime who was guilty by association. Instead, he asked that whatever unsettling punishment was waiting for us around the corner of judgment be swift.

His merciless side began stockpiling his weapons of resentment toward me for getting sick in the first place.

I disrupted his plans for a future to buy a bigger home, fancier automobiles, and all the worldly possessions that our salaries could purchase. How dare I extinguish his fire to acquire! In sickness and in health, it was my duty to please him and fulfill his every whim and desire. Inside his imperfect imagination, he demanded nothing less than perfection from me. During his cheap and cheating courtship, he told me that he had found the ideal wife and woman of his dreams. Like him, in the beginning, when I only saw him at his best, I idolized him. I convinced myself that I couldn't live without him. And the possibility that I might not be able to have him made the candy even more enticing. So now that the genie of love had granted me my wish (which was based solely on selfishness without regard for anyone caught in the crossfire), karma was sure to show me what happens when I failed to live up to, or interfered with, his avaricious pursuit.

Julia and Jay sat by my bedside for the next two hours, which really made Arthur uncomfortable. This wasn't because he didn't like them. Rather, it was because having any part of my family around disturbed Dr. Jeckle's schedule and congenial bedside manner. He was tired of containing his unpleasantness and being forced to entertain them with pleasantries.

At eight thirty in the evening, a nurse came in to check my vital signs. "Visiting hours are over. The IV has a tendency to make bladders work overtime, and the instructions are not to let her out of bed until morning. She will probably need to use the bedpan often, so it would probably be easier on her if one of you can stay."

Jay kissed me on the cheek while I laid motionless. "Good night. I love you. I'll try to come by tomorrow night." The nurse walked out with Jay.

Julia said to Arthur, "I can stay. I know it's been a long day for you. Why don't you go home and get some rest?"

He politely answered, "Thanks for offering. But I'll be fine here. I'll just ask the nurse for a pillow and a blanket. I can sleep in one of these chairs. Besides, you have a family to take care of."

She repeated, "Are you sure? It's really no bother. I can spare to lose a few hours of sleep. I don't have a job to go to tomorrow. Brian can stay with Justin until I go home in the morning."

He insisted, "I appreciate your kindness, but I can't let you do that. We'll be fine here. Maybe when she comes home, you can help her then."

He was one for trying to make a good impression, and he felt awkward because he had only just met her earlier in the day. Even though I heard them both, he spoke for me. I wished intensely that Julia could sense my quiescent attempt to beg her not to leave me alone with him. I sensed from his tone that he still hadn't developed a cell of compassion for what I was going through. The effects of the anesthesia lingered. I was too exhausted and in too much pain to anticipate what he was going to say or do to me in my vulnerable condition.

Hours later, while Mr. Hyde had been resting quietly in the shadows of another, waiting to emerge from underneath the covers, the morphine that I was given for my pain wore off, and nausea set in. Nearly every half-hour from then on, he was awakened by my need to urinate. I held off my request to use the other bedpan the nurse had left nearby (for retching) for as long as I could. But then I begged, "Arthur, please. I can't fight it any longer. I'm dizzy, and I'm going

117

to throw up."

He threatened, refusing to take the bedpan off the table and give it to me. "It's just your nerves. If you don't straighten up right now, I'm going to leave you here all alone! Quit being a baby and take it like a soldier!"

After I coated the sheets and myself with stomach bile, I asked, "If you really didn't want to be here with me, why didn't you let my sister stay?"

Before he could answer, the nurse came in to strip the bed and clean me up. "Poor baby," she said sympathetically. "You're having an adverse reaction to the anesthesia. It's common. It will pass after it runs its course." I wanted to tell her to send him away. I stopped myself, reasoning that at the moment I was completely and totally at his mercy.

When the nurse left the room, he answered my question with all the cruelty inside of him. "I never even met your sister, and you expect me to ask her to stay here with you, like I'm an incompetent idiot. Your sister only showed up out of guilt, not because she loves you. If you would've died during surgery, she would've never been able to forgive herself. She was only here for her benefit—not yours." His previous threat to leave me all alone only reinforced what I was already feeling. As I tried to travel back into dream-land, this nightmare I was living resonated a familiar form of cruelty that happened years before.

Because Helen lacked the attention of her biological father for years, the child in her was always craving it. She often went out of her way to keep the attention on herself and not on us. She played on Father's guilt of his first wife being a woman who was physically ill often, but he never took Mom's complaints seriously. So when Helen couldn't compete with his distractions—like his flock—she enlisted the attention of anyone who wasn't familiar with her antics.

One night, when gout was her latest ailment, she blended up a parsley, carrot, and celery juice mixture, serving it with dinner. She was told by some retired chiropractor in the congregation that if she drank the juice mixture, it would cure her. If she had to suffer, we all had to suffer. She filled our glasses to the brim with the juice. Father went around the dining room table with a belt in his hand. He threatened to spank anyone who didn't finish all of it. When I started to retch, he came over to me. "Drink it, or I will whip you until you do!" I focused on the red-and-white velvet wallpaper that layered the upper half of the dining room wall, while the bottom half of the wall was covered with walnut paneling. I tried hard to redirect my attention away from the awful taste and texture of the mixture. My hands were shaking, and I was unable to keep the slimy substance in my stomach. I regurgitated back into the glass. I saw the sternness in his eyes as he moved closer and waved the belt in front of my face. He forced me to drink my own vomit.

It seemed that the mental excursion down the streets of my tormented childhood was a premonition of what I was in for if I didn't change directions. I was praying that God would let me heal quickly and make the vertigo subside. But mostly I prayed for salvation out of the hands of the devil who was parading around as my husband. I made a promise that I kept to myself. If I made a full recovery, I was going to leave him and file for divorce.

With the morning came a new day. I was anxious to hear an encouraging report from Dr. Epstien. His smile was friendly and his touch was compassionate as he changed my bandages. He checked my pupils, tested my hearing with his tuning prong, and had me move the muscles in my face. Then he gave his prognosis. "Everything looks very good. There's no facial nerve damage, and your hearing is already showing some improvement."

"What about the vertigo?" I asked.

"Are you experiencing it now?"

"I don't feel as bad as I did before the surgery. The room isn't spinning. But I'm not up and moving around."

"Follow my finger." He placed the tip of his forefinger on the tip of my nose. He then held his finger up and moved it out away from my nose—from side to side—and finally back to the tip of my nose. "You still have nystagmus. You may be experiencing it because of the swelling after surgery. I'll prescribe an anti-inflammatory, which should help. It may take a couple of weeks before you notice some improvement." He began making notes on my chart.

"What if it doesn't go away?" I asked.

"We'll have to do more testing." He looked up and turned his attention toward me. "You're a very lucky girl. It could've been much worse. We caught the infection in time, before it had a chance to spread. You could've gotten meningitis at anytime during the last several months. During the surgery, I replaced the tube that I put in your ear when I drained it the first time with a new one. So your ear will continue to drain for awhile."

"So do you think the infection caused the vertigo?" Arthur asked.

"It could have. Or it could have been caused by something else. Shoshanah, do you remember when I told you that the eardrum was abnormally tilted?"

"Yes."

"Did you ever go skin diving while you felt the fluid in there?" he asked.

"No. I swim, but I hardly ever go underwater."

"What about flying?" he asked.

I gave Arthur an irritated look. "As a matter of fact, I did. I didn't think it was a good idea, but *my husband* insisted."

"We had to go," Arthur said. "My cousin was getting married. It was only a two-hour flight. It's not like we went around the world on the Concorde."

"It doesn't matter," he said. "The high altitude puts pressure on the inner ear. That could've caused the eardrum to recess inward."

"But if the fluid inside was from an infection and not from an allergy, wouldn't that do harm?" Arthur asked.

"Yes, if it's left untreated. Another possibility is that it could have started out as an allergy or cold and then turned into an infection."

"So antibiotics, or getting a tube put in earlier, could have prevented this?" Arthur asked.

"It wouldn't have hurt."

Though I knew the answer, because I had asked him before and now I wanted Arthur to hear it first-hand, I asked the question again. "What about cats? I know I'm allergic to ours."

"You might want to consider getting rid of it or trying shots. The worst is over. Now let's hope for the best."

Once Dr. Epstien left the room, Arthur said, "Well, honey, I think I smell a malpractice lawsuit."

"You heard what he said. I should've never gotten on that plane. And I should've made you go to Paul's wedding by yourself."

"I told you before we left to go and get it taken care of."

"I did. It's not my fault that the doctor didn't drain my ear."

"Then you should've gone to another one," he said.

"And when was I going to have the time to do that?" I asked. "The more doctors I went to see, the more you accused me of being a hypochondriac. And if I'm not available to work the mandatory overtime, I'll lose my job."

"Christine and Kurt will never let you go. They just gave you a bonus and an award for being employee of the quarter—remember?"

"Things change rapidly there," I said.

"If you can sue that other doctor, maybe you won't have to worry about it."

"Maybe. All I know is that we have to get rid of Sheba. I'm not going through this kind of pain again."

"I've had Sheba since Elaine and I got married. She was with me first." He might as well have told me the truth—his cat came before me.

12

I was being rolled into a coffin headfirst. The plastic MRI tube resembled a cannon and the inside of my head an artillery shell. While a pulse of radio waves that worked in conjunction with a magnet produced pictures of the fragments that remained from the previous massacre, I was instructed to lay completely still. With my world spinning out of control, I had to stay calm and watch everything I had worked for die a slow and painful death.

It had been eight months since an alien entered my body and held me hostage on a frightful freight train that led me down the tracks of hell. The infection was gone, but the damage it caused was irreparable. The intense vertigo persisted with a vengeance, as did the nausea, vomiting, and the inability to drive or function without extreme difficulty. Experiencing continual vertigo was like being stranded on a boat in the middle of the ocean, and I was being navigated through treacherous waters with a constant rocking motion. The periods when I was floating on calm seas were brief. It was only when I laid with my head elevated on two pillows while remaining stationary that I encountered these temporary moments of relief. Any kind of upheaval or any activity involving much movement, and I was battling stormy currents. If anything within my peripheral vision was in motion, such as my being a passenger riding in a car and staring out the window at the scenery as I passed by, it would induce an attack. Seeing objects move stimulated my optic nerves and triggered impulses from my inner ear. These, in turn, were transmitted to my brain. As a result, the sensation I experienced felt like an uncontrollable force that was pulling my body to the left, leaving my sense of balance off kilter. I truly knew what it felt like to be a drunken sailor lost at sea.

After my mastoidectomy, I continued my follow-up treatment with Dr. Lucos and not with Dr. Epstien. Dr. Lucos was trying to find a resolution for my bewildering medical condition. But he was also milking it for everything it was worth. Every orifice of my body was inspected, practically every vein pricked, and nearly every drop of blood carefully inspected. In the past six months, two internists, one neurologist, and two neurotologists had examined me. And so that I left no stone unturned, I also sought another opinion from a specialist at the Mayo Clinic in Jacksonville.

My day-to-day existence was like living inside a nightmare. I was getting fired at from every direction. Once I regained consciousness after a hit, and I was trying to salvage any of the remains of my life, another grenade would get thrown in my direction. I was so busy doing damage control that I didn't know where I was half the time. I was walking a thin line, wobbling in between sanity and periodic thoughts of suicide. Everything I had worked to achieve for most of my adulthood was destroyed in a matter of months, and the rest was on the brink of destruction. The only peace I found was when I was sleeping, so I slept a lot. Whenever I retired to bed and before I drifted off, I prayed for a miracle. When I arose and discovered that my medical condition hadn't disappeared or improved and I was still living inside the nightmare, I cursed God for being alive and waking up to face another day of hell. Over the past several months, I was slowly withdrawing from everything and everyone.

When Arthur refused to drive me to take another MRI, I was forced to drive myself. So I had to forgo the antianxiety drug that was prescribed to me, which would have made the experience less frightening. In my condition, I was already putting other motorists at risk. But if I were to get caught behind the wheel while under the influence of mild sedation, I would have gambled with the possibility of getting my license suspended. Then I would really be trapped and totally dependent on him. He guised his agitation by claiming that if he were to take the morning off to drive me to my appointment, it would jeopardize his job. Doing so would appear as though he were abusing his privileges in his new position.

Despite the poor example of marriage that I witnessed and the lack of proper parenting skills that I was a victim of, my ideals and priorities were altogether different. I always envisioned marriage as being an equal partnership where one mate comes to the aid of the other, especially in times of crisis. Out of love, I imagined drawing strength from my other half. Out of hatred, I made a daunting discovery. In my darkest hour and when I needed him most, he proved that I couldn't rely on him for support. The longer my condition showed no signs of improving, the threat of losing our material possessions became extremely real. It seemed like for every corner I turned, there was another mountain for me to climb. I was strapped to a harness that was trapped inside a body of limitations. I reached out for his hand many times, thinking he was a link of support. I made a habit of disillusioning myself that he would help pull me back up to the top where I belonged. Yet as his intimidation increased in my vulnerable state and my fear heightened, I became aware that he was the one shredding my lifeline. The only thing I could depend on him for was resistance.

Once the test was complete and the technician was confident that the pictures were clear enough to read, I was free to go. I went searching for answers and comfort from a source that never let me down.

Sophie was standing in front of her favorite Jewish delicatessen, The Bagel's Ganaiden. Since her retirement, Sophie seemed to be aging rapidly. The last time I saw her was shortly after my surgery. Because my condition restricted me to driving only when there was no other alternative, and Sophie's vision was declining and she no longer drove after dark, we relied heavily upon the telephone lines to keep our connection alive.

"Sorry I'm late," I said. "It's difficult to plan anything on the same day that I'm scheduled for any doctor's appointment. I never know when I'm going to get out of there."

"There's no need to explain, darling. You're talking to a pro. During all the years that I've been *sleppen* this old workhorse around, I've had almost every test under the sun." The minor bow in her back, caused by the osteoporosis that was settling in, paid homage to the baggage she was referring to. "I thought Arthur was coming with you."

"So did I, until last night. Apparently, there's some project that he needs to finish."

We sat in a booth next to the window and placed our orders before getting into any serious conversation. Sophie started, "On the one hand, I'm glad he didn't come with you today. If he had, it wouldn't have given us the opportunity to visit. But on the other hand, I'm concerned. You really shouldn't be driving in your condition. You should've called me. I would've taken you."

"I know. Forgive me for being a *draikop* [a scatterbrain]." She smiled affectionately at me. "It's just that I haven't been thinking clearly since this whole thing started. And besides, you know me. I'm just like you. I hate to be dependent on anyone."

"Well in times like these, you need to know that you can count on me . . . and your husband. It sounds like he needs to get his priorities straight."

I tried hard to brush his disregard for me aside. "He's been very busy since his promotion."

"It sure was different in my day. Men shouldered their responsibilities and took care of their wives. If they didn't, they were reproached and run out of town. In my opinion, Agent Orange must have crept in and damaged the semen of those fathered after World War II because I've never seen so many *parechs* in the generations that followed."

"Refresh my memory. What does *parech* mean?"

"A low-life man."

"Nothing ever turns out the way you expect it to," I replied in a melancholy tone. "And when you think you know someone, it turns out that you really don't know them at all."

"Are you referring to your husband?"

"No . . . never mind." I quickly changed gears. "How's your family?"

"Everyone's fine. No major catastrophes to report." The waitress came and served us our lunch. I took a couple of bites from my corned beef sandwich and pushed the plate to the side. "What's wrong, darling? Aren't you hungry?"

"I guess I'm not as hungry as I thought. I'll take the rest home."

"You're looking too *svelte*. You need to eat. Your mother, *oleho hasholem* . . ."

"May she rest in peace," I repeated.

"She isn't here to dote over you, so you'll have to settle for me."

I took a few bites from the coleslaw and then nibbled on the dill pickle. "There, is that better?"

"Listen, darling, I'm not trying to be a *kibitzer*, but this is Sophie. You can't fool me. There's something troubling you. My mind isn't as sharp as it was when we met. My eyes are failing me, but I can still hear pretty well. I'm just as good a listener as I've ever been. It will do you good to let it out. Holding it in will only do you more harm."

The bags underneath her eyes and the thick lenses of her eyeglasses were symbolic of her experience in being precisely perceptive. I was doing a poor job of masking my befuddled state. Because I made light of my dilemma since I became ill, she was under the impression that at Arthur's request I had taken a leave of absence from my job. I felt another attack coming on, so I took out a Valium, broke it in half, and swallowed it. The pill medicated my misery and knocked down any walls of apprehension I had in telling her the ugly truth. My anxiety and uncertainty had been mounting, and the emotional valve needed to be released. I held nothing back, knowing that if I expected her to offer me any sound solutions, I had to be completely honest with her.

Once my employer discovered that I wasn't improving after my surgery, they let me go. I was learning that loyalty in the workplace was history. How quickly they forgot the time that I was the only employee who volunteered to work third shift before it was enforced. This was so that the company would win a bid on a lucrative contract. Without the manpower and extra shift, they wouldn't meet the deadlines, and without the contract, the company wouldn't have any other choice but to start laying off some employees. But just like a lot of other people in my world, when it came time for them to reciprocate courtesies, they had nothing but excuses to offer. They covered their ground legally, laying off two other employees at the same time. I questioned what prompted the sudden change in my employee value. Then I argued that I had experience in all of their software programs— unlike a few who were spared. To no avail. I was told that I was chosen because I was married. (So there was someone else to support me.)

When I lost my job, the umbilical cord that was nurturing me was severed. I had become a hollow tree because of Arthur's constant pecking away at my self-esteem. Losing my job was just the beginning. I was pushing back the hands of time, with the months counting down to when my health insurance and unemployment benefits were going expire. Once my COBRA coverage expired, I was uninsurable for my present medical condition. No company was going to insure me because of my preexisting condition. This, and my ability to foresee a grim future if my present condition prevailed, sent me into a whirlwind of anxiety. The medication that was alleviating some of my symptoms had short-and-long-term side effects, not to mention that it left me in a lethargic and sluggish state. So not only was I unemployable, but I could forget about leading a normal life again. Additionally, since our financial resources were completely depleted, any expenses that were above our normal living expenses were being paid with credit cards. Because he was the major breadwinner, I felt like my fate literally rested in the hands of my enemy.

After the shock dissipated and my senses were restored following the layoff, I called Dr. Lucos's office, insisting on an appointment. I was planning to explain my plight to him. I assumed that my predicament would send a bolt of sympathy his way and would evoke him to take action. I hoped that he would either recommend another procedure that might improve my condition or send me to someone more specialized in his field who might know something that he didn't. He had an enormous ego and a short fuse of impatience and intolerance for any woman who was in an emotionally fragile state. My angst over having not one ounce of control over my situation caused me to be irrational at times, and my way with people often lacked tact. Consequently, I couldn't make his nurse understand that medically speaking nothing had changed and I was simply requesting an appointment to speak to him. Finally, she said that she would have him return my call. One day later, when he didn't return my call, I called his office again, trying for a second time to get through to the nurse. I made the mistake of communicating my concerns to her. This infuriated him, and he instructed his nurse to tell me to continue taking the Valium that he had prescribed.

Ten minutes later, I received a telephone call from Arthur, who was at work. "Well you've really done it this time. When will you ever learn to lay down and shut up?"

It was common for him to call me every afternoon since I stopped working, so I wasn't taken aback by his call. But I was dumbfounded by his question. "What are you talking about?"

"I just received a phone call from Dr. Lucos."

"Oh, I see. You're good enough to talk to, but he refuses to take a phone call from his own patient."

"What did you do to piss him off?" he asked.

"Nothing. I wanted him to return my call. Why? What did he tell you?"

"He's threatening to have you admitted to a psychiatric ward," he said.

"On what grounds?"

He raised his voice to a subdued screaming pitch. "What do you mean 'on what grounds'? You idiot! Have you ever heard of the Baker Act?"

"No," I answered in a browbeaten tone.

"If you're depressed and suicidal, which is how he claimed you were acting, he can place you into a psychiatric ward for observation."

"That's funny. He didn't even speak to me. But I get the picture now. If I don't shut up and take drugs, he's going to have me locked up. Yet he's the one who's prescribing the drug that's known to be a downer. Not to mention that depression is natural for anyone who's sick and unemployable."

"Quit talking like you have a paper asshole! He's in control—not you."

After I served him dinner that evening, I took a walk around the neighborhood to try to clear my head. When I returned home, the front door was open to the inside, allowing the breeze to pass through the screen door. His voice echoed off the tile floor and through the hallway. I followed it down to the den, which was in the back of the house. The door was shut, which was usually an indication of one of two things: either he wanted to read in peace and quiet, or he was having a private conversation on the telephone. On both accounts, I was not to disturb him.

He was reiterating the conversation he had earlier with the doctor, embellishing it with profanities. It didn't matter whom he was talking to because I focused only on the words that made me wish I were deaf. "I'm not staying married to an invalid. She's useless since she came down with this illness. And now that she's lost her job, all she does all day long is sit around and worry. Her unemployment benefits run out in two months. What am I going to do then?" A few moments of silence passed. Then he continued, "Oh no I won't. I learned the first time around. I'm not going to be the loser again. I'll do whatever it takes to hang on to this house. It's the only thing I've got." A few more moments of silence and "ah huhs" later, "If I divorce her in the condition she's in now, I'll probably have to pay alimony. My only alternative is to make her miserable enough so that she'll get fed up and leave." Then he chuckled, adding, "It's tempting, believe me. Why do you think I make her vacuum the pool every day while I'm at work? The neighbors would never see anything with a seven-foot wood fence in the way. A drowning happens all the time down here."

The booby trap blew my mind to bits. Eavesdropping on his blitzkrieg was devastation enough. But when I stepped on another land mine, the blow knocked me to the ground. With my back literally up against the wall, I gradually slumped down onto the floor. If I was going to survive, I had to shut off my emotions, not letting him sense that I was on to him or make him aware that I knew his agenda. I had to hurry to my feet, watch my enemy closely, and prepare for his next plan of attack.

The following day was Saturday. These were set a-

132

side for doing household chores. I usually spent most of the day cleaning, doing laundry, and grocery shopping. But since I became sick and had time on my hands, I did a little of these activities each day. He spent his Saturdays working in the yard and doing maintenance on our vehicles or the house. I was relieved when he decided that he was going to devote most of the day to pressure cleaning the roof. It made it easier for me to stay out of his way.

To avoid our cars getting hit with any of the debris, he moved his truck out of the driveway and in front of the house, along the swale. He asked me to move mine there as well. I followed his orders. However, my ability to judge distance accurately was off. Hence, the tires on the driver's side were on the pavement. Before I got out of the car, he came out from behind the screen door and motioned for me to park the car all the way inside the swale. I didn't argue, knowing that the other cars that were passing by might hit it. When I put the car in reverse, I hit the mailbox. He came stampeding over as if he were a bull and had just been let out of his pin, with bloodthirsty horns aimed directly at me, his target.

"What are you doing idiot? Turn the wheel!" The belligerent badgering reinforced my nervousness. I cut the wheels the wrong way, and the metal box scraped across the rear door on the driver's side. "Not that way, you stupid woman!" When I got out of the car to see how I needed to maneuver the wheels, the mailbox was dangling from the post by a couple of screws. I briefly glanced across the street. Some neighbors were watching us. I rushed back into the house humiliated, with the raging bull on the foot of my heels just waiting for me to stumble. I was trying not to provoke him further. As I sensed what was coming yet was uncertain how far his rage would take him this time, I felt my blood pressure rising. He slammed the front door shut, prohibiting the neighbors from listening. He shred me to pieces, tearing me up one side and down the other with his razor-sharp tongue. When I ignored him, by pouring a cold drink, he grabbed my arm. I pulled away, dropping the tumbler. As I cleaned up the broken glass off the tile floor, it was all I could do not to lock horns with this bullheaded Taurus. "You never pay attention to what you're doing. What were you thinking?" I neither answered nor looked up. "Answer me!"

"I said I was sorry. It's only a scrape. It's my car, and it's not worth getting all worked up." I emptied all the shattered pieces, *of the tumbler, that is,* into the wastebasket.

He then transformed himself into a drill sergeant. He came within an inch of my face, using his intimidation tactics to wear his plebe down. He looked me in the eyes and said, "That's not what I want to hear, you piece of shit!"

Though I wanted to give him a dose of his own poison, I contained my anger, terrified of the reaction it would generate in him. Instead, I concentrated on not giving him the satisfaction of bringing me to tears. "You promised that you weren't going to say those words to me ever again. I want an apology."

"No, now tell me why you ran over the mailbox!"

I became frustrated. "It was a mistake. I didn't see it. What else do you want from me?" He picked me up by my upper arms, holding me up just long enough to look me in the eyes again and spit on me. "Put me down. You're hurting me, and you're deliberately trying to hurt my feelings."

He put me down, after which he started squirming his body around like a worm while he remained standing. "Feelings, feelings. You women always want to talk about feelings. Get your head out of your ass! If you would quit worrying about your fucking feelings so much and concentrate more on what you were doing, this wouldn't have happened." I finally realized that it was pointless to discuss anything with him while he was in his drilling-and-rage mode. I walked away and into our bedroom. I was filling a duffel bag with clothes when he came into the bedroom and continued to stab me with his words. "Poor Shoshanah. She can't take the pressure because she's nothing but a fucking piece of shit! You're dumber than my asshole!"

While he was attempting to assassinate my soul, I figured out that he wasn't going to stop until I gave him the response he was hungry for. As he moved closer, tears poured out of my eyes and my hands shook with fear. Though he had won, I was still determined to hang on to an ounce of dignity. I zipped up the duffel bag and said, *"Me ken kush in toches arein!"* [You can kiss my ass!] I felt safe cursing him in Yiddish.

"What kind of shit are you mumbling?"

"I'm tired of being treated like garbage."

He ripped the bag from my hands. "You're not going anywhere. You don't have anywhere or anyone to run to. Where are you going to go—to your father? Huh! He doesn't want you! No one wants you! You're becoming a pain in the ass to everyone."

I left and drove around for a few hours. I drove over to Jay's house, but no one was home. I headed for Sophie's but soon remembered that she was visiting her son in Miami. The stress from his interrogation aggravated my vertigo even more. I didn't want to risk driving anymore. I could get pulled over or into a traffic accident. My shame in the choice that I made, by marrying a completely compassionless bastard, kept me captive. When my defenses and rational returned, I went back home. I was haunted by the words I overheard the night before, when I eavesdropped on his conversation. I was wondering how close his aggression was going to push him toward becoming more physically violent. My iron will refused to give in to his monstrous methods, leaving him with everything. Yet the longer that I stayed, I was falling further into denial. *If my condition would improve, then he would treat me better. He's only acting out of fear. If this illness doesn't destroy us, then perhaps it will make our relationship stronger.*

Like always, he apologized, making promises that his own sickness wouldn't allow him to keep. "Don't you see? One of us has to stay strong. If I become as weak as you, we're going to sink." He seemed to have no control over his tongue, just as I had no control over my emotions. I knew that there was some measure of truth to his words, perceiving that he was just as terrified as I was about the future.

The damage was done. No explanation he offered me could penetrate the wall that he was making between us thicker, the same wall of terror I grew up with. I was flooded by repressed childhood memories. I never thought that I would have to use the same coping mechanisms with the man I married. I became a good silent soldier again, taking orders and completing the list of duties that he had prepared for me every morning before he went off to work. It was a list not much different from the labor list that Helen, the warden of my childhood, prepared for my siblings and I. I became a slave under his totalitarian reign.

I looked into Sophie's sympathetic eyes that wept for me since mine remained as dry as a desert. Numbness had settled in to quench my thirst for tears. She shook her head in disgust, then said, *"Sara groisser potz!"* [What a big prick!]

"I don't understand where I went wrong. I didn't get married just to escape the house I grew up in. I waited until I was mature, and we lived together for six months before we got married. I thought I did everything right."

"There are no easy answers. Right now, all I want to do is choke the son of a bitch, but that's not going to solve anything. First, don't rock the boat anymore than it already is. Unfortunately, he's in control because you aren't able to earn any income right now. Stay out of his way and make yourself scarce. Second, why don't you try applying for disability benefits?"

"I already checked into it," I said. "The company offers it, but they're never going to admit that's the reason why they let me go."

"Forget about them. Check with Social Security."

"You know, that's the cruelest irony of it all: to be the only one in my family who finished high school without taking a short cut [getting a GED]. Then I even went on to earn some kind of a degree. Yet I'm the only one to be stricken with an illness. God rewarded me for being ambitious with a kick in the gut."

"He does have a sense of humor," she said. "But he's not to blame. If anyone's to blame, it's Arthur."

"You're right. Being forced to take his shit, it's a miracle I haven't blown my brains out."

"Don't talk like that!" There was silence for a moment as I stared blankly across the room. Then she took off the necklace she was wearing. The pendant sparkled in the afternoon sun, like gold dust floating through the air. "Lean forward, sugar. I want you to wear this." I hesitated. "Don't worry. I have a spare, but this one is special—like you."

"It represents the hand of God, right?"

"Yes."

"What's special about this one?"

"I got it over in Israel years ago. May it bring you good luck."

I hugged her. "Thank you. A *schlimazel* like me could use some right now. Could you put in a word with the man upstairs?"

"You haven't had it easy. Since I've known you, you've had to swim up stream just to survive. But what doesn't kill us makes us stronger. The good Lord brought you this far. You can't give up now. If you get on disability, you won't have to take Arthur's shit anymore. You know my door is always open to you."

"I know. I just never expected things to turn out like this."

"This too shall pass. You'll see. And the sun will come out again." She opened her purse and took out two wrapped pieces of chocolate. She offered me one before eating the other. "I need this like I need a hole in the head. When you get to be my age, you learn to enjoy the simple pleasures. They can take away my red meat and coffee, but I'll never give up chocolate."

A few days later, I took Sophie's advice and contacted Social Security. If I was found eligible, there was a long waiting period before I would be able to collect any benefits. I didn't know how I was going to tolerate six more months of my painful existence. After I finished talking to an administrator, I threw the telephone receiver against the wall. I went searching through every room of the house, looking for my little girl who appeared the day when I received the call of death. But I guess she was afraid of the dark, or she was too sick to come out and play. The sobs that had brought me to my knees earlier had carried me into bed. My despondency was draining every cell of inner strength I had. In a moment of psychosis, I literally felt a sharp fingernail go up my spine and a voice tell me to kill myself. It felt like the devil's chains of oppression, which were wrapped around me, tighten, and I contemplated turning my prison camp into a death camp. I remembered what I was taught as being the punishment for suicide. I imagined demons below me laughing as they threw more brimstone on their fire. I'm sure some angels above blew kisses in efforts to blow out the devil's flame, and my soul was for hire somewhere in between. Clutching the chasma, I begged for deliverance from my evil assassin. "Oh, Mommy, I'm so frightened of the darkness. I need you. Please help me!"

The wicked whispers telling me to take my own life were hushed by heaven's dialogue: *My precious Peaches, I'm so sorry I'm not there for you. I was only a channel by which you were to travel. I cannot live your life for you. I can only guide and watch over you. My absence is to make you stronger. Fear in living will only make you more fragile. Now go and know that I'm so proud of you.*

The words strengthened me. It was then that I made the choice to live and fight with everything inside of me. I made a pact with God and my lost soul. I promised never to betray my feelings again. If God healed me enough to break free from Arthur—the mortal that I thought the devil was using to rob me of my soul—then I would find a way to help others. I didn't know how or through what means I would be asked to do so. I merely asked that God show me the way and I would follow.

My search started by yielding to my intuition and allowing it to guide me. I scheduled an appointment with Dr. Epstien within a few days. After I explained my trying circumstances, he told me about a renowned specialist in Nashville who possibly offered a solution. If successful, a procedure involving an intracranial procedure, where sections of the vestibular nerve are severed, could alleviate most of my symptoms. This prospect kept me going for the next six weeks until I was fit into the specialist's schedule.

While Arthur attended Mass, holding his rosary and hailing Mary, I wore the chasma and reached out for God's hand to pull me out of my darkness. I allowed my unwillingness to forgive Arthur's hypocrisy divide us in our worship as well as in our bed.

13

As Arthur and I left our hotel on the outskirts of Nashville, we took the expressway and headed for downtown. The humming of wheels spinning against pavement and the motion of the windshield wipers hypnotized me. Late-summer rains began to mystify me with trickles of times past. I was holding a silver pendant of Mother Mary, the latest souvenir that Ilona had given me, which reminded me that she was the closest I had ever come to having a mother again. I tucked it inside the sleeve of my Bible along with a photograph of Mom, and I held all three close to my heart. Covered with this breastplate of armor, prayers for protection guided me into a few unconsciousness moments, and I felt heaven's umbilical cord nurturing me across the miles. If mortality knocked on my door, I was hoping on a hereafter, where I would cross paths with Mom again.

As a child, I questioned what happened to Mom after she died. Of course, I had already been conditioned not to put myself or her in the context. So, I used the scenario of asking Father what happens to *any* person after they die. He explained that the deceased one doesn't go to heaven or hell. They are in a deep sleep waiting for Christ to raise them from their tombs (exactly as they were before their death) after Armageddon, when the wicked are cleansed from the earth. If someone died before they turned thirty, then after their resurrection they would progress in age until they were thirty. If someone died after they were thirty, then after their resurrection they would regress in years until they turned thirty. Additionally, any who survived Armageddon would regress or progress to this age, and the aging process would cease thereafter. Then they would dwell on a paradise earth as perfect inhabitants. *Such a lovely fairy tale, and Father always accused me of being a dreamer. I guess the founder of the cult forgot to factor in the dilemma of over population.*

The idea that I would be able to see and touch Mom again in the flesh someday sounded wonderful—until I learned that she would no longer be married, and she wouldn't be allowed to remarry after her resurrection. I remember asking, "When the dead people come back, aren't they going to be sad when they see their husbands or wives married to someone else and they-'re not a family anymore? Won't they cry because they're all alone?" I refused to accept how a god could be so cruel to bring Mom back to life with the same human feelings and desires as she had before she died, but she wouldn't be allowed to act on them. Even then my precocious mind wasn't buying into the gibberish.

Better still was the guilt that the belief instilled in me if I bought into it. Father frequently played on this prior to and following my escape. The threat was always looming that if I were wicked and failed to survive Armageddon, I was never going to see any friend or loved one again.

After a few hours of extensive testing, Arthur and I met Dr. Soros. Once we exchanged pleasantries and he examined me, he said, "I can see from your records that you've seen a number of specialists."

"She does get around," Arthur added.

"I apologize for making you take some of the

tests over again. Before I could give you my diagnosis and offer any recommendations, I wanted to be sure that all the tests are current."

"Whatever it takes," I said. "I just want this nightmare to be over."

"So your symptoms are aggravated by any activities that require you to move around a lot, such as running, riding a bike, or climbing stairs?"

"Yes. I haven't been able to do anything like that since I got sick."

"How about driving in a car or plane?" he asked.

"We drove here," Arthur said. "The trip could've been done in one day, but I didn't want her in the bathroom for the next two days vomiting."

"And how about when you lie down?" he asked.

"It's not as severe as when I'm moving around. But I still feel like I'm on a boat."

"Have you noticed any difference right before your menstruation begins?" he asked.

"It's a little worse. Since I've reduced my salt intake, I've noticed a slight difference."

"Good, that's important," he said. "If you just had vertigo that comes and goes, I would say you have Ménière's disease. But because your symptoms persist, and the results of the Ménière's test that you had this morning and previously are negative, it's impossible for me to make a conclusive diagnosis."

"Are there any procedures that will help?" Arthur asked.

"Since water retention effects your condition, my first recommendation would be endolymphatic sac surgery." He went on to explain in detail one other procedure. But because the diagnosis was unclear, there were no guarantees that either surgery would improve my condition—and both were temporary solutions. (For example, the shunt that's used in the sac's surgery would have to be replaced in a few years.) He concluded, "If you like, I can schedule you for surgery at the end of the week."

"I appreciate your opinion and taking the time to see me," I said. "But I don't have the luxury of waiting to try one procedure, and then if it doesn't work try another one. I've lost my job. I can't work, and the COBRA insurance that I have is only temporary. Without being able to earn a living, I don't know how much longer we can keep paying the high premiums. Once I lose my insurance, no doctor is going to touch me in this condition. What happens when the shunt needs to be replaced? By that time, I won't have the insurance I have now, and no company is going to insure me for a preexisting condition."

"Dr. Epstien suggested a vestibular nerve section," Arthur said. "That's really why we came all this way to see you. He told us that people come from all over the country to see you because you're the best in your field, especially when it comes to that procedure."

He smiled. "That's true. I usually do two or three of them every week. I haven't mentioned the nerve section because it's quite an intensive procedure. And the risks involved are greater with that surgery than they are with any of the surgeries that I've mentioned."

When I recognized the dreadful tone that's used whenever a bomb is about to be dropped and devastation is just around the corner, my shoulders dropped. "I'm willing to take those risks," I said.

"What risks?" Arthur asked.

"It's minimal, but there's potential for total hearing loss, facial nerve damage, a stroke, or even death. I don't usually perform this procedure on someone so young, especially when the test results aren't conclusive. The procedure is also irreversible. Once sections of the nerve are severed, there's no turning back. Most of my patients have success with it. But in this case, it could worsen her condition."

Arthur asked me, "Wouldn't you rather be in this position than wind up with one side of your face paralyzed—better yet, slip into a coma?"

You would love that, wouldn't you, you son of a bitch? You wouldn't wait two days before you had them turn off life support. Then you could cash in the one-hundred-thousand-dollar life insurance policy that you have on me. I heard the demons trampling down the hall in their death march, and I sighed. "So it's not an option."

"I sympathize with your situation. But I have to take the most conservative approach at this time. If you want me to help you, then I have to exhaust all the other options first. I'll leave you two alone to decide what you want to do. I have to go check in on a surgery that's being done at the hospital across the street. I'll be back shortly."

As Dr. Soros walked out of the room, it was as if I stepped outside of myself again, renouncing reality. Five minutes passed in silence, though I could find no peace inside my mind, for the powers that be had forsaken me once more. Arthur rambled on, but I couldn't tell you what he said. Locked in the fight-or-flight position, my only alternative was to become paralyzed by panic. "I just can't believe that God would have us come all this way for nothing," I said. The voice of a lunatic interfered with my intuition; it was Father. *It was to build your hopes up so that we could dash them one more time.* His demonic laughter was working diligently to drown out the power of positive thinking.

"How do you know this isn't God's way of telling you to back off? Maybe something terrible will happen if you have the nerve section."

"I know the shunt won't work. Even Dr. Lucos didn't think it would. What am I going to do? This is the end of the line for me. I can't live like this anymore."

The devil, who had his claw around my neck, was beginning to strangle me. Arthur raised his voice and attempted to drive a nail into my coffin. "Just kill yourself!" Arthur said. "Do it, and put me out of my misery! I'm sick of listening to you. I just wish you'd get the fuck out of my life!"

While my muscles winced with every whimper, a waterfall of tears came gushing down my cheeks. I held the chasma pendant that Sophie had given me and prayed silently with everything in my soul. An army of angels flew to my rescue. It was the most fleeting time of suffering I had ever experienced. God's hand was mightier than Satan's grip.

When Dr. Soros returned, he said with bewilderment, "I'm not a religious man. But while I was in the operating room, it was as if someone had spoken in my ear and told me to reconsider my decision." He looked into my eyes and smiled. "Someone upstairs must be looking out for you," he said.

"Does this mean that you're going to do the nerve section?" I asked.

"Yes, but only as long as you agree to go through a few days of positional rehabilitation. I have to justify my decision with your insurance. Since this procedure involves a craniotomy, a neurosurgeon will also be involved. I want you to be aware that this operation is not a cure. If it's successful, you will experience a great deal of relief from your symptoms. However, you're never going to function exactly as you did before you found yourself in these unfortunate circumstances."

"Then what's the point?" Arthur asked.

A bolt of energy zapped through me, immediately lifting my spirits. It was as if an angel handed me a weapon to fight with. I rose up out of the coffin, pulled out my spiritual sword, and placed the tip of it under his chin. *Don't even think about it. I'm taking back my power.* "It's my only chance to have any kind of life again, and I'm taking it—with or without you."

Dr. Soros looked at Arthur, waiting for his rebuttal. But he remained silent. "Okay, then. I'll have my nurse make arrangements for you to consult with the neurosurgeon, Dr. Johnson." The angels untangled the evil chains that were wrapped around me, and the demons disbanded. Resting on the wings of seraphs, I was on my way out of exile.

I made it through the surgery without any complications. However, nothing within my vision was motionless. In fact, it didn't matter if I was standing, sitting, or reclined, the vertigo was worse than before. I feared that Arthur's negative projection was right. Thankfully, another one of my prayers was answered when Dr. Soros assured me that it was to be expected. Patients usually felt worse until the inflammation subsided and their central nervous system adjusted to running on one engine—so to speak. Time would only tell if it was worth taking the risk. There was no turning back, and there was no procedure or medical protocol beyond this point.

As soon as my condition stabilized, Arthur returned to Florida. The break from him was refreshing. My mouth watered at the appetizing thought of the peace that was mine when and if I had the courage to make my way out of the forest. If something didn't change, I knew that my physical health would never improve. Prior to the post-traumatic Arthur period, my only hospital stay was for a tonsilectomy. Since my encounter with the big bad wolf, however, I was gathering quite a collection of battle scars. He called a few times. But I felt it was more to inflict guilt on me, over the new set of medical bills that were already arriving, than anything else.

When I was moved out of the intensive care unit and into a regular room, my in-laws added a colorful cast to the flavorless sodium-free meals and the boring sport of channel surfing. Shortly after my sponge bath in the mornings, they would show up and keep me company. I was rarely a whiner or complainer, except when I was sick. My hyperactive side didn't make for a good patient. I hated being a convalescent. Though I never whimpered aloud, inside I was bawling like a baby for Mom or Nana. My surrogate mother was just as good as the real thing. Ilona didn't hold any of her maternal instincts back when it came to nursing me back to health. Likewise, in order to prevent blood clots, I gratefully accepted and looked forward to my walks on Andras's arm around the corridors three times a day. Whenever we returned to the room, Ilona was there fluffing the pillows and smoothing out the sheets. Then she would tuck me in, and as Andras told me stories, I would drift off to sleep. Spending time with my in-laws made me forget the silver-tongued devil whom I was married to. It made it difficult for me to imagine how my cold-blooded husband came from such loving parents. As always, the bedtime story ended too soon. Before long, the trip to grandmother's house was over.

A week following my surgery and the morning that I was released, my bandages were removed. When

I held a compact mirror in front of me and looked into the bathroom mirror to see the back and side of my head, nothing could prepare me for the grotesque incision I saw. Andras and Ilona did their best to reassure me that it was only hair. It would grow back, and once it did, any scars wouldn't be noticeable. My departing gift was a plastic bag containing eighteen inches of my tresses and a personal hygiene kit. It was the only downside to the procedure that caused me sorrow. My hair was the longest it had ever been, taking five years to reach the middle of my back. Ilona gave me a scarf to cover the trail of symmetrical staples, which ran from the left temporal to the left occipital portion of my scalp.

A flight attendant pushed me in a wheelchair up the boarding ramp. I waved good-bye to the possibility that I might be leaving a bittersweet part of my past behind. Andras and Ilona stood gazing out of the airport terminal window until the DC-9 backed up and was cleared for the runway. I sat hidden behind my scarf of seclusion, feeling as though all eyes were upon me. I had done everything within my power to improve my condition; the rest was up to heaven. I tuned out the wolf's howling that echoed off the coral reefs of the Atlantic and all the way across the Tennessee Valley. Instead, I tuned into the lullabies that were serenading me from cloud nine. I erased the image of being a lost little girl again who had to go off into the dark forest to face him all by myself. I closed my eyes and began to create more illusions to inspire me.

Shortly after Arthur picked me up at the airport, my optimistic outlook waned. My most recent disillusion, where he was concerned, was that somehow all the turmoil that we had been through had softened him. Then my shield of defense could slowly come down and I could let him in again, especially since, just days before, my first Social Security check arrived in the mail. Even though I was no longer his cash cow, the pressure was off him to be the sole supporter. Between being tired, suffering from airsickness, and the car ride home, I felt as though I had just come from a wild, spinning ride at an amusement park. I didn't fight it, nor did I cry. I closed the pocket door to the guest bathroom almost completely, except for a crack, and laid on the floor resting amid periods of retching. Despite my attempt to keep my malady a secret from him, as if I were doing something wrong, the big bad wolf came looking for me anyway. I was too weak to run, so once more I was forced to accept his unwarranted punishment. It had been nearly a month since he had me all to himself and without any disruption in his daily chastising feast. The beast was on the brink of starvation. I saw his beefy frame standing in the doorway. His look of disgust was cold reality slapping me in the face for the five-thousandth time. "Here we go again," he huffed.

Apparently, he still had a demon sitting on his shoulder. He quickly forgot the time before we were married when he had pneumonia. I lovingly bathed, dressed, and hand-fed him in bed because he was too weak to walk to the kitchen table. Yet he couldn't return one cup of that compassion to me, even though I had been through so much more. His cruel gesture made me grateful, for the first time in our marriage, that I didn't have a child with him. If I had, I would've had to shoulder the responsibility alone. It would've been a constant battle to kill or surrender to those destructive feelings that make a child feel like a burden. The same burden that I was made to feel like when I was a child. Between Father's ego propelling him into trying to create a nation because he couldn't rule one and his refusing to use birth control, his wives had to bear the consequences of his selfishness.

Father heard about the surgery through Jay. I was home only a few days when Helen called and asked if they could stop in for a visit. I was so miserable in my present situation that the old wounds from the past were buried deep in denial. Their concern led me to believe that perhaps they would offer me the love and compassion that I wasn't getting from Arthur. I played my sympathy card, envisioning time mellowing Father and that the religious reins that empowered him were loosening. Therefore, his empathy over what I had endured in my life could seep in and show him that his priorities were grossly distorted. And because they were gracious enough to send us one hundred dollars as a wedding gift, when they heard I had married, gave me hope.

When they arrived, Father handed Arthur the latest issues of the *Watchtower* and *Awake* magazines and Helen greeted me with a carnation. Just as Father's main method of communication was through his religious propaganda, Arthur's was in drawing attention to another person's weakness. I was resting on the couch and watching television while he showed them around the house. Then they came into the family room to join me. Arthur walked over to me and lifted up the strands of hair that I had combed over to one side of my head (in the same fashion when a bald man brushes the few remaining long strands of hair over the top of his head). He made a spectacle of the staples that had not been removed by Dr. Epstien yet. "I've given your daughter a new nickname, Zipperhead,"

Arthur said.

I guess Father couldn't resist the temptation to dip his tongue into the fountain of psychosis that seemed to be overflowing in the room that night. "I told Jay the illness was all in your head, and it was." I got a flash of what it must have been like for Mom having to live with an insensitive imbecile at times. I recalled what a therapist had told me about history repeating itself. I made a mental notation: *not if I can help it.* I had plans to rewrite history just as soon as my health improved. The chapters to follow in my book of dreams, which I had yet to fulfill, didn't include either of these men. Rather, the only significance these two had was absolute eradication, particularly on how to identify and warn others of villains like them. Hopefully, one day their kind will become extinct and eventually the good apples will outnumber the rotten ones.

When all the pretenses were out of the way, Helen nudged Father with her foot. I interpreted this as a signal expressing that she wanted to leave. But he went on to reveal the real reason for their visit. "You hurt Helen and I by not telling us when and where your surgery was going to be. If Jay wasn't working for me, I'm sure that I probably would've never heard the news. We heard Arthur's parents were there." He had a lot of nerve making a statement like that, because the last time he saw me was months earlier, shortly after my first surgery. He called once thereafter but hadn't called again since then. In large part, I always held Helen responsible for the lack of concern. If it wasn't for the tragic turn my life had taken in the past year, I might never have seen Father for the pathetic person he was. Because a loved one in his past had hurt him, he had become a hardened criminal when

152

it came to matters of the heart.

When the kindness and generosity of my in-laws made him look bad because he had allowed religion to come between blood, I, his dead daughter, was suddenly resurrected. He quickly revealed his latest bait: to fuel my false hopes so that I would get back into the ring just long enough for him to knock me down again.

"Arthur's parents were there because I wanted them there," I replied. "They paid for most of our traveling expenses and came to visit me every day. Without their help, taking the trip would have been almost impossible."

When he didn't get the apology that he usually got from me in the past and realized that his power over me was disintegrating, he wanted to leave. He had no desire to stay when things weren't going his way. "Well, deary, I hope this operation worked better than the last one."

Time hadn't changed anything. Helen and Father were still acting as if they were the wounded ones. They suffered from selective memory syndrome, disregarding the fact that if they wanted the respect for being parents, then they had to act like respectable parents—not vacationing visitors. Much to my dismay, this was yet another delusion that I had to let go of: *Daddy isn't going to come and rescue me.*

The gigantic boulder to awaken my subconscious was only the beginning. The palette of truth foreshadowed the dark side of Arthur and overshadowed the shady side that Father was hiding. The countdown was on as to when I would be autonomous over both men.

14

The summer season blended into the amber brush of fall, and the leaves of misfortune began to sashay away. Winter winds blew over the portrait of my soul, defining its depth and divine purpose. While cradled in God's hand, I spent six months building up my physical stamina. Bathing in spiritual healing waters and enveloped with the comforting revelation of the Creator's eternal love, I was testing the strength of my wings. With the days of spring fast approaching, I charted my course on a path of new beginnings.

Meanwhile, it sickened me every time I had to sleep with the enemy. Though I told myself that I was forced to give myself to him in order to keep the peace until I was strong enough to flee, I felt like I was forsaking my soul. After I became limited in my earning potential, he seldom took to sexually pleasing me. I had grown tired of hearing him complain whenever I made any oral requests to receive some kind of pleasure out of our physical union. Before long, I learned that solitaire ensured me a winning hand, whereas playing poker with the devil only guaranteed another losing streak. When we did have sexual relations, it was always according to his timetable of passion—not mine—which was usually once or twice on the weekends. I detested him so much that as soon as he was done pleasing himself (I didn't refer to him as the sixty-second man for nothing!), I wasted little time in getting up and dashing into the bathroom. Then I looked at the semen he had ejaculated into me as it fell into the toilet bowl. But I didn't see seeds of reproduction; I merely saw venom falling from my womb. My stomach muscles heaved in apprehension at the thought of what was to come if my methods of birth control failed. If he impregnated me, I would be chained to him forever. So, as I often watched the potential for his maliciousness to mutate—and breed another misogamist—fall from my womb, I worshiped the porcelain base. I prayed, asking that I pass through another ovulation cycle without getting pregnant.

I respected the doctors' honesty and did not set myself up for disappointment by having unattainable goals, such as returning back to work immediately. They reminded me that any surgery on the body is considered trauma. And because the muscles and nerves in my head and neck were involved, it could take up to a year before the weakness, and my susceptibility to getting fatigued easily, would subside. It would also take my central nervous system some time to compensate my body's musculature to maintain equilibrium. Quite often, during my healing and recovery stage, whenever I laid down to rest in the afternoons, the inside of my head felt like it was vibrating. I wondered if this was from the drilling that took place during the surgery. I remembered coming out of my heavy sedation slightly while I was on the operating table. I heard the voice of Frank Sinatra playing in the background, and I was dreaming about being at my in-laws' house. Then I heard someone utter, "She's starting to wake up." With that, I was out cold again. As a result of the vestibular nerve being intertwined with facial and hearing nerves, it was impossible for the doctors to sever it completely without causing permanent damage to both. Therefore, I continued to have bouts of vertigo. But at least they were just bouts; instead of the constant merry-go-round that I was on before. I still had minor nystagmus, which meant that any rapid eye movement, such as reading extensively or working on a computer, exacerbated my condition. Likewise, stress, fatigue, inclement weather, being afflicted with a cold or the flu, and traveling inside a moving vehicle for long periods of time induced further episodes. Fortunately, these were tolerable and only temporary.

I knew that I wasn't well enough to return to work as long as I was in the healing stages. What I was most grateful for was that I was able to function without medication. The drugs I had been taking previously altered my moods, and if they were used on a continual basis, had serious side effects. I slowly emerged out of my denial phase and was gradually accepting the fact that I wouldn't be able to return to drafting or the field of architecture. Yet I needed to return to some form of employment to give me a sense of accomplishment and boost my self-esteem. But most important, I needed to gain independence from the big bad wolf, because the disability income wasn't enough to support myself.

It had been nearly a year since I was on any payroll. If I was ever going to join the workforce again, I knew that I needed to get back into the mode of being productive beyond my domestic capabilities. The first place I thought was a good start was inside a class-room. In a sense, I was learning to crawl all over again. It would take additional strengthening of my mental processes before I felt confident enough to go on a job interview. Perhaps if I could manage one class, then I was on my way toward earning a paycheck again. The discipline needed to accomplish the assignments would give me direction, purpose, and structure. Eventually, when I discovered which tasks I would be capable of handling and which ones I would not, it would lay the groundwork for a new career. From there, I could determine which career goals would be within my reach.

My first baby step was toward picking a subject that I knew came easily to me so that I wouldn't set myself up for defeat, therein squelching any ambition I had to continue. I selected English, a core curriculum course that I previously excelled in. When I made an A on my first essay, which had to be completed in class, I came home excited and proud. Instead of receiving any praise, Arthur asked, "Is your teacher a man?"

"Yes. Why?"

"That's why you got the high mark." He was devouring the few scraps of encouraging nourishment that I was so desperately famished for. This was a reminder that even though he was no longer cursing profanities at me, he was still working diligently to devalue me in any way possible.

His insensitivity was reminiscent of a time when I was a high school sophomore. As is common in most households, Father and Helen demanded to see my final grades at the end of each nine-week period. For two consecutive periods, I earned a perfect score in all my subjects. No, I didn't get rewarded with any money or special privileges. Rather, they simply dismissed it as if it was an everyday occurrence. Yet, bringing home any mark less than a C was grounds for punishment. It seemed like they looked for any excuse to punish me, especially Helen. Similarly, when I was a junior in high school I won third place in a state spelling competition. I brought home the trophy, waving it in front of them, always looking for a scrap of approval, especially from Father. The only words he could come up with were, "That's nice."

I had finally come to the sad conclusion that I married my Father. As long as I didn't do anything to have an identity outside of being a wife, I wasn't a threat to his manhood. *After all, as a woman, I was put on this earth only to serve men's every desire, whim, and need.* Arthur was licking the icing off his fingers, for he thought that he could have his cake and eat it, too. He had me right where he wanted me, under his thumb and dependent on him. He was in hog heaven, rolling in the mire, thinking that he had it better than most control freaks. His victim stayed home with no contact to the outside world while continuing to bring in some sort of income. It was irrelevant how the resources were coming in as long as it was enough to keep our home, enable him to buy a new vehicle every two years, and take an extended weekend trip to see his family twice a year. He was dancing with devilish delight, thinking that he had gotten away with another attempt to murder my soul.

His insulting remark was certainly less degrading than what I had encountered in the past. And during the last six months, his behavior had switched from unpredictable raids to an occasional demeaning shower. Regardless, it was the straw that broke the camel's back. I had had enough. I knew that the drop in his temper was only temporary, until another stressful incident occurred when the beast inside couldn't be contained anymore, and it would emerge again. I took advantage of the cease-fire, tucking away any money that I could, contemplating what I was going to do for my survival once I left him. As the semester ended and I earned a perfect score in my class, my days of remaining his prey were numbered. His birthday was approaching, and I was going to make it a farewell feast that he would never forget.

I fixed a pot roast with all the trimmings and a special dessert with a blast from the past. I was going to give my anal retentive husband a flaming end to our marriage. I was gloating inside as I served him his second helping. The poor *schlemiel* was going to have a restless night with the sting of retribution burning him from the inside out in ghastly explosions. I invited, "Honey, save room for your dessert."

He was gorging on two large brownies topped with vanilla ice cream that were covered with chocolate sauce. "Where's yours?" he asked.

"Chocolate has caffeine, which is one of the no-nos on my diet. It could set me into a tailspin." *And with any luck, you too.*

"I forgot," he commented sarcastically. "You can't take a shit without consulting your doctors first."

I laughed inside among my thoughts. *By the time you finally climb off the toilet seat, Mr. Wonderful, you're the one who's going to need a proctologist.* I waited until his belly was full before I gave him his due. "By the way dear," I handed him a birthday gift, "I'm moving out tomorrow. I want a divorce."

"Don't tease me."

"Oh, I'm very serious," I said.

He rose from the chair. "What?" he screamed. "Things are just starting to settle down. Why do you have to rock the boat now?"

"Because . . ."

He cut me off. "I told you I was sorry about how I treated you before. It's been months since I've called you names. What else do you want from me?"

"Nothing." I stayed calm, refusing to raise my voice. "You've done enough damage. I just want what's mine. And then I want to be left alone."

"You'll never make it on your own." It infuriated him that his permanent punching bag wasn't going to be around anymore. He took his belt off, and as he began hitting the kitchen countertop, he shouted, "You bitch! Of all the times, how could you do this to me on my birthday?"

Though he tried to intimidate me, I didn't flinch—at least on the outside. But inside, I was petrified. I resisted the temptation to grab the belt from his grasp and strangle him with it.

He stormed out of the kitchen and went into the garage. When I heard the side door leading out onto the backyard slam, I knew that I had a few minutes to run to safety. I went into our bedroom and took his scouting knife out of the nightstand drawer. As I walked to the guestroom, I folded a pillow in half, shoving the knife in between. When I saw him in the backyard shouting out loud as he shut the sprinklers off, I trembled lightly. A few minutes later, the big bad wolf banged on the door and puffed, "Open up, or I swear I'll kick the door down!"

When I didn't verbally respond to his threats, he returned with a screwdriver. I was dragging the dresser in front of the doorway when he jimmied the lock and burst in. He grabbed me by my arms, picked me up, and threw me on the bed. The room started to spin a bit, and I was getting dizzy. I laid my head on the pillows. Then he picked me up by my arms again. He began shaking and knocking my head against the pillow, using one of Dr. Epstien's warnings to his advantage. (If I shook or bumped my head while I was in the healing stage, it could cause brain damage.)

160

His fangs were now in full focus. "God how I want to bash your head in right now!"

"Go ahead and kill me! Prove to me that I'm not making a mistake by getting out of this marriage. If you kill me, you'll go to prison. If you beat me, I'll file a report. Then the court will give me everything."

He stopped shaking me, but he was still on top of me, and he pinned down my hands. "You're the one who wants the divorce, so you're the one who's going to suffer. I'm not moving out."

"I didn't expect you to do the right thing. That's why I'm going to leave."

He threatened, "You're not going anywhere. Your name is on the mortgage as well as mine. You have to stay here until we can sell this house. And since the houses aren't moving in this neighborhood, you'll be here for a while."

"Hell, for all I care, you can foreclose on this stupid house. I've lost everything else—what's a house? You're the one who insisted that we had to buy it."

"And you're the one who got sick," he said. "If you walk away, I'll get you for abandonment."

"Sorry I messed up your plans. This is a no-fault state when it comes to divorce. All assets get split up fifty-fifty."

"Yes," he said. "But whatever equity we had in the house was already used when we took out the loan for the pool. There hasn't been enough time to recoup it."

"I'm aware of that. But we have two pension plans."

"You bitch!" he screamed. "Those pensions are mine!"

"Fine. Then I want the fifteen thousand dollars that I came into the relationship with, most of which went into this house because you didn't have a dime. Don't you remember? You were in debt."

"You can't get it if I don't have it. There's not enough money in our savings account for you to scrape up the money for first, last, and security on an apartment."

"That's what credit cards are for," I said.

"Oh no you don't. Most of those are in my name. There's only a couple that are joint, and I'll cancel them as soon as they're paid off. And no company's going to hire you in your condition. You'll never make it."

"Watch me," I said, as the ten laxative tablets I had melted into the brownies and chocolate sauce finally took effect, ensuring me a peaceful night's sleep. He jumped off the bed and ran into the bathroom, where, for a change, he was the one seeking refuge inside the toilet bowl. The refuse was pouring out of his rectum, where it had belonged all along, instead of defecating the portals of my psyche. I was relieved that I didn't have to use the knife. I knew that he was capable of being a dragon just like Father, and watching him pelt the countertop transported me back in time to a day in my childhood that I thought I had long since forgotten. The memory was resurrected, and the wound was just as fresh as it was then.

Most of the time, Father's behavior was predictable. As I got older, I was able to sense when the emotional volcano that was brewing inside the dragon was going to erupt. His mood was usually contingent upon what was going on in his environment. If things were going well, business was booming, and my siblings and I were seen and not heard, he was pleasant. But if things weren't going well, particularly with his business, he came home disgruntled. He lacked the discipline to separate his family life from the stress that his business put him under. He also lacked this quality when it came to his children and his relationship with Helen. There was often a strong parallel between his fights with her and his angry outbursts.

Helen had a shorter fuse than he did, and it didn't take much to provoke her. She openly displayed the distasteful mood she was in. On the other hand, he let his madness fester until it came to a boiling point, and then he would explode, many times into a rage. When the two had been fighting, the dragon came out of his dungeon swinging his tail at any of us that were in his path. Helen could take care of herself. She made it clear that if he ever laid a finger on her, she would report him to the elders, which would put his position as an elder in jeopardy. She also threatened to leave him (she did on a few occasions but always returned within a day or two) to raise *all* his children as a single parent.

Whenever I got hit with the belt and the monster inside Father appeared, he was satisfied enough in giving me between three to five licks before retreating back into his dungeon. But after my older siblings got their "get out of jail free" card, I was the last to receive the brunt of his unresolved issues. So on this particular day when I was sixteen, he was unusually possessed and unable to suppress his demons of the past any longer. That's when a man, who hid behind his Bible and professed to walk with God, took a diabolical detour. As he drove me into darkness, I became his helpless passenger.

Father was taking us home from another Sunday meeting. Helen was sitting up in the front seat of the van brooding. I was in the back with my younger siblings. He said something that I wasn't clearly able to make out. She ignored him, turned her body away from him, and stared out the window. He reached over and put his hand on her knee. She abruptly pushed it away and turned her nose up in the air. She crossed one leg over the other and jiggled it impatiently. Her sour demeanor evoked a dreaded feeling in me—that either my siblings or I were going to be on the receiving end of the wrath that she roused in him. My stomach churned with every corner, and I nervously chewed my fingernails. (A habit formed out of fear, which stayed with me until I escaped from their childhood prison.)

Once in the driveway, Helen got out first and slammed the door so hard that it shook the van. She tapped her foot on the front concrete step like a child, waiting for Father to unlock the front door. "If you don't take care of this now, there'll be no nookie-nookie tonight," she threatened. (When it came to Father, sex was her most powerful weapon.)

Moments later, I was in my bedroom changing into a terry cloth robe when Father stormed in. The dragon inside him quickly emerged. He didn't spare me a second to replace the soiled sanitary napkin I had just disposed of. He pulled me by my long locks and drug me through the family room and then through the kitchen. I saw fierce gloom frozen on my siblings' faces, like they were just as terrified as I was of what was to come. Helen smirked at my terrorizing moans.

He dragged me to their bedroom and slammed the door shut. His nostrils flared and evil fumes spewed forth. He snarled, "Sister Fuller told Helen at the meeting this morning that you refused to go to work for her because Helen had gotten you the job. She also said that you told her that we are rotten parents!" (Mary Fuller was an older woman in the congregation who did massage therapy and reflexology out of her home.)

"No I didn't," I replied meekly. "I only said that I didn't want to work for her because I don't like doing reflexology." He slammed me up against the wall. My heart thumped, and I began to tremble.

It was like spitfire was coming out of his mouth. He screamed, "You're a liar, and you're going to pay for it!" Then, instead of hitting me in the traditional way with the belt folded in half, he held the belt as a single strap. The buckle fell to the end like a weight on a whip. With this, he pelted me. One strike, two strikes, five strikes more.

The metal was digging into my flesh, and blood began seeping down my legs. "Stop! Please stop!" I begged. Six and seven strokes more! "Why are you doing this to me, Daddy?"

He looked into my eyes. But I don't believe it was me he saw. In order for me to pardon his beastly behavior, I have to believe that he saw his deceased wife's ghost gazing back at him. Perhaps the demons inside his head were cursing her for abandoning him and forcing him into the miserable existence his life had become. He hated her for dying and killing his dreams. More so, he hated her for the guilt he was reeling with for not paying more attention to her when she was alive. Though the deepest hatred—I think— was for Nana. Her poltergeist voice may have been badgering her accurateness about Helen's wickedness in his ear with another 'I told you so.' He briefly stopped, pulling the crown of hair on my forehead. His brown eyes were blazing as he answered, "You have the same poisonous root that my mother had, and I'm going to beat it out of you!" A poisonous serpent might as well have injected me with deadly venom, because those words nearly destroyed my psyche.

I was writhing on the carpet for reprieve from his reprisal, trying to dodge his tail. When he kicked me in the back and abdomen with his boots, my body jerked. Then he switched back to pelting me. He stopped beating me only long enough to walk over and open the door. "Helen, come in here!" I placed my hands on the edge of the bed, trying to pull myself up. My limbs were raw and stinging. He kicked me back down to the floor and pulled my hair. "Now, I want you to beg for Helen's forgiveness! Beg, I said!"

"Please forgive me Mother," I moaned.

She laughed, then scoffed, "I just can't take this," and she walked out of the bedroom.

I started to get up. "Where do you think you're going, young lady? I'm not done with you yet!" He continued to degrade me with his acts of dehumanization for the next few minutes.

As I hobbled back to my bedroom, I passed through the kitchen again. I noticed that my siblings' gloom were replaced with tears of sympathy and dread, as they probably wondered if their souls were next in line to be exterminated.

I cleaned myself up and laid on my bed. I was stunned by fear, and my limbs trembled uncontrollably. My body had become a traumatized vessel at the hands of my own father. There seemed to be no antidote for his lethal injection. Nor was there any escape as I came to the desperate realization that I was all alone. The voice inside my head was asking, *Why God? Why doesn't anyone love me? Surely, you have abandoned me also.* That was a turning point in my young life when I realized that I had no one to depend upon but myself. All my allies were gone, and my younger siblings were just as vulnerable to his evil as I was. I made a promise to myself to save every penny that I earned working. Then, on my eighteenth birthday, I would flee. From that time onward, I knew that I had to kiss both their asses. My craft at cunning them into thinking that I was going to become the perfect soldier had to be flawless. Otherwise, if he suspects my disloyalty—I thought—he may kill me. Because I had never seen him so much out of control, I was also afraid of being burned at the stake.

The Witnesses derived their mind-twisted doctrine from the Puritans. In order to expel the demons completely, they were admonished to literally burn anything that they thought to be possessed. Because I was raised in a sheltered environment, I didn't personally know of or hear about any child like me, who was being held hostage by an abuser in the name of religion. The closest mental assimilation I had been exposed to were the documentaries I had seen about the Holocaust in school and in watching the miniseries *Roots*. Though I knew that my suffering didn't even come close to those victims, from that day forward I had a difficult time differentiating between a fanatic like Hitler and Father. It was because my impressionable intellect couldn't have conceived, let alone accept, that the man who assisted in my creation could treat me like a slave.

I was still crying ten minutes later when he burst in. "What do you think you're doing? You're not a queen! Now get out here and fold laundry." I walked out to the family room and sat down beside Kara. My hands were shaking as I bent my arms in discomfort while the welts of wrath formed. I was folding a towel when the intimidating trepidation that he saw in my face made the power-hungry maggots inside him feel like a *real* man. He had his belt in his hand, this time folded

167

in half. I flinched with fear and almost jumped off the couch. The dragon snorted, as he hit me again, "You aren't folding fast enough!" he screamed.

Two hours later, in all his sanctimoniousness, he slipped into his God-like complex. A committee meeting, where he was to sit as one of three councils, had been arranged. An imperfect man—who in my eyes had become a torchbearer for the devil by placing the chains of evil around his own daughter's neck and doing irrevocable damage to her soul—was now going to decide the spiritual fate of a confessed sinner. His opinion was taken into account of the ultimate decision as to whether the person would be disfellowshipped. Before he left the house, he went back into my bedroom. I was inside my closet contemplating running away when he ordered, "Give me your car keys and your savings account book." Then he threatened, "If you tell anyone—including Jay and Julia—or if you run away, you'll get it worse when I find you and bring you back." In those days, there were no automatic teller machines. If there was HRS, I certainly wasn't aware of it. I knew that with only the twenty dollars I had on me I wouldn't get very far. If I had taken advantage of the choice I had just months before, I might've been able to avoid the dragon's doomsday blitzkrieg.

For most teenagers, turning sixteen was celebrated with parties or gifts. However, in our house turning sweet sixteen meant that we were required to pay rent. Fifty dollars a month wasn't an exorbitant amount. But as a child still in school, where was I going to come up with money unless I worked? Also, in efforts to keep us from being influenced by anyone outside the cult, we were given this ultimatum: drop out of school and go to work full time or drop out and become a pioneer for the cult. In effect, I was forced to preach the gospel that promised paradise on earth while living a lie with a hypocrite.

While most teenagers loathed school, I cherished the hours inside the classroom. I excelled in most of my studies. So school not only provided a temporary escape route, but it also gave me confidence. Determined to graduate, I was able to compromise with him by enrolling into a work program where I went to school for a few hours in the morning and then went to work in the afternoon. But as I laid in the trenches and was digging my way into paranoia, I regretted not dropping out of school and working full time. If I had been able to save enough money, I would have been long gone.

Since I knew that he was going to be gone for the next few hours, I decided to try to talk to Helen. To prevent it from repeating, I wanted to understand why I got the beating. I was honest with him. I never said any of the things I had been accused of saying. I also needed to know the next phase in my enemies' attack so that I could stay one step ahead of them and spare my life.

The door to their bedroom was open. I walked over to the bed, where Helen was reclined watching television. "I'm sorry for whatever I did. But I swear I never said those things about you and Daddy." I started to whimper. "I've never seen Daddy this angry. I'm afraid he's going to kill me."

She took a stroll with the dragon down Lucifer's lane. The evil torch was burning behind her eyes as she laughed. "He's not going to kill you. You had that beating coming to you. You deserved it. I read your diaries, remember? I know how you feel about us."

It was on behalf of sustaining my sanity, still having

two years left to serve of my prison sentence, that my subconscious didn't allow my conscious mind to accept the truth until years later. If I had realized that Helen fabricated the story, which in turn fueled Father's rage, I may have been serving a *real* prison sentence for murdering the witch. Then perhaps her conscience would be clear for not committing the crime against me herself. After all, it would quiet her insecurities of living with any of Mom's ghostly remains.

The episode Helen was referring to happened a few weeks before. She went snooping through my dresser drawers and found my diaries. I hid the keys underneath the inside sole of a pair of sneakers that I hardly wore. But this didn't stop the dragon's double from slicing open the jacket to each diary and reading them while I was at school. After dinner that night, I was summoned into their bedroom. She sat in a corner pouting, acting as though she was the one who had been wronged. My diaries were open and laying on the bed.

The mighty dragon said with cold-blooded composure, "We haven't decided on what your punishment should be. The things you wrote about Helen and I aren't true. You have a very sick mind, and you're obviously obsessed over your dead mother. We want to be sure that no one knows how crazy you really are. I want these diaries destroyed. I want you to go in the backyard and burn these on the grill. Then I want you to bring me the ashes. This will teach you to never write about things that you have no business expressing your opinion on. You don't have a voice. Oh, and another thing, since you like to write so much, I'm giving you until tomorrow night after dinner to write five hundred times, 'I don't have a voice.'"

Helen had become the dragon's mistress. She stood behind her evil assailant. "It's eight o'clock now. Lights are out at ten. After you finish with the dishes, I suggest you get started. We wouldn't want to keep you from your writing."

I was forced to watch my feelings (my inner being) go up into flames. They raped my soul and stole my greatest coping mechanism, my inner voice. I, an aspiring teenage poet, went into hiding, refusing to pick up a pen for several years. And from that point forward, any happy memories of my childhood were eclipsed by that traumatic event. Moreover, secondary to my trepidation, that Father's psychosis could propel him into committing homicide, was that I would go insane. Thus, my only sane approach left was in resorting to imaginary figures and plays inside my mind. These illusions involved real people in my environment. They became heroes and heroines who rescued me from the stark reality that my life immured.

After my fight with Arthur had jolted me into the past, and I returned to the present, it was the first time I understood the impact that Father's crime had had on me. Unfortunately, I was at an age when the petals of adolescence start to open. Just as I was on the verge of blossoming into womanhood, the root of my essence had been damaged. I remained limp, crushed inside, never given the chance to bloom because the weeds that surrounded my stem blocked out any sunlight. So, not only did Father take the scripture "spare the rod and spoil the child" to an extreme, but he might as well have thrown me a shovel and told me to start digging my own grave. All my future prospects of having a positive relationship with the opposite sex were going to be buried there. As each negative experience left its signature of death on the tombstone, Father was named as the assassin. Coming so close to reliving that trauma again with Arthur only reinforced my need to build a barricade around myself. This was in order to preserve my wounded ability to trust any man. I had no control over Father being in my garden in the first place, and I couldn't undo the damage that Arthur had done. I became painfully aware that both men came from the same contaminated stock. It was up to me to make sure that neither of them succeeded in trampling me to death.

15

I said in a shell-shocked stupor, "So even though I'm classified as disabled, I'm not entitled to alimony. And he doesn't have to pay me back the money that I invested into the house."

The third divorce attorney whom I had consulted in the past two weeks for free advice replied, "I didn't say that. You're entitled to a lot of things. Nevertheless, between the mortgage, his car payment, and whatever other incidentals he has, it doesn't sound like he has any money left over at the end of each month to pay you back. And you can't get blood from a stone."

Everyone was quick to voice their opinion, and I heard it from both sides. Some friends and relatives said I should walk away and forget about material possessions; others said I was a fool if I walked away from my house, the only weapon I had left to fight with. Now it seemed that I was being forced to surrender it over to my enemy without just compensation.

"What about the pensions?" I asked.

"You're entitled to half of those. But you may have to wait until you reach what's considered the average age for retirement before you can draw on it. At which time, the amount will be based on how long you two were married."

"That's not going to do me any good. I need the cash flow now."

"You can always wait and buy time," he said. The real estate market could turn around, and maybe your luck will change."

"My luck ran out the day that I married that asshole. The only way I would go back into the devil's triangle is if I were packing a pistol, so that the next time the douche bag decides to threaten me it will be his last." Before I lost my way in the forest and took up with the big bad wolf, my use of profanities was limited. But now, I was building quite an extensive vocabulary. My soon-to-be ex-husband had a habit of bringing out the ugliest emotions in me.

"Here's my card. If you want to use my services, my retainer is one thousand dollars to file the paperwork."

Though his second marriage was coming to an end, Arthur refused to file for divorce. I believe this was for two reasons. The first one being: he didn't want to give the appearance of being reckless by not taking his marriage vows seriously. He also didn't want to be perceived as a cruel and tactless prick who was taking advantage of me in my seriously disadvantaged position. I wanted to believe that if his parents knew the truth, they wouldn't have been so eager to give him the financial support that helped him maintain his lifestyle.

The disgusting truth was that he threatened that if I didn't quitclaim the deed of our house over to him and relinquish all rights to alimony, then he was going to tell Social Security that I had been working part time to supplement my income. Though this was permissible, I had been doing it for the past six months off the books and without their knowledge. I never wanted alimony or the house. I just wanted to be compensated fairly for being mistreated so badly that I was left with no other alternative than to walk away.

The second reason that I believe why he refused

to file was based on his experience. Having gone through a divorce once before, he knew that whoever filed usually had to pay for it. If I ever wanted to collect on anything that I was entitled to or sever any joint financial obligations that bound us, I had no choice but to file. It was sadly ironic that the money I was fighting for was exactly what I needed to fight for my entitlements to begin with.

The disability income that I was receiving was only a third of what I had previously earned when I was working. I was grateful for the help, yet I felt ashamed because I never had to rely on public assistance before. Fortunately, federal policies allowed me to subsidize this income by working part time. I wasn't allowed to gross over five hundred dollars a month, and the employment could be in any field as long as it wasn't related to my previous one. If it was related to my previous field, then I wasn't allowed to gross over two hundred dollars a month. Thus, I returned to cleaning residential homes on a part-time basis. There was subsidized housing in my area, but there was a two-year waiting list. Additionally, I still had almost a year left before I was eligible for Medicare. Though I was no longer under constant medical supervision, I still needed health coverage, which had nearly doubled since I lost my job. Based on these two fundamentals, working part time wasn't an option, it was a necessity. Once Medicare began to kick in, I had a year to breathe easy until I was up for my medical review. As far as Social Security was concerned, my medical condition was slightly unpredictable. Though it was less likely to improve, there was a chance that it could, just as there was the possibility that it could deteriorate. If they felt I had improved, I would receive three months of severance pay and they would close my file. There were no guarantees, especially in my life. I had to have a plan to re-structure my life that would also improve my financial situation.

Jay offered me a place to stay indefinitely. I had never been a freeloader, and my pride wasn't going to let me even contemplate turning into one. I intended to take advantage of his offer only until I could save enough money to file for divorce and get into an apartment of my own. This worked out well since we were both separated from our spouses. He and his wife, Sheila, were ending their eighteen-year marriage. They decided that it was best for their two teenage daughters to stay with Sheila, while Jay had sole custody of Avery, their five-year-old son. Jay had to be at his job site early in the mornings. Therefore, getting a kindergartner off to school was difficult. Since Jay refused to take any money from me, we worked out a mutual agreement. In lieu of paying rent, I was responsible for getting Avery ready for school—taking him there in the mornings and picking him up in the afternoons—and baby-sitting him until Jay came home from work. Then when Jay returned home, I was off to class. This arrangement enabled me to put some of my resources toward continuing my education. Until I knew exactly which career path I wanted to take, I abstained from applying for any school grants or loans.

I never imagined I would fall in love with Avery in such a short period of time. From the looks of things, it was hard to tell which one of us was becoming more attached. He had become a welcome diversion to my recent turmoil and brought out all the maternal in-stincts that had been latent in me.

My day began with an early awakening by his cracking open my bedroom door and poking his head inside. The dread of being abandoned is probably what bonded us more than anything else. He stuck to Jay like a pin. So when Jay had to leave for work before the sun came up, he cuddled up to the next-best thing. I would pull back my covers, inviting him to rest beside me, while I tried to stroke away his insecurities and answer his countless questions. Then my gentle demeanor had to turn into tough love over breakfast and the morning cartoons. It was a challenge of time management to get him bathed, dressed, and pack his lunch in time for school.

Several months following my last legal consultation, I was sitting in an office at the courthouse signing the divorce decree. Arthur didn't bother showing up, but he might as well have been there holding a gun to my head. "Are you aware of your rights?" the judge asked. While my heart was bleeding and the pain of injustice was seeping from every chamber, I nodded. I had promised myself that I wasn't going to get the short end of the stick, but Arthur continued to have the upper hand. The deck was stacked against me, and I was stripped of all my artillery. I had no weapons to fight with, and he knew it. The hungry beast residing in him, who had no conscience, was doing his best to eat me alive anyway. If I had not been aware that I was entitled to half the pensions up to that point, he wouldn't have had to compromise or offer me anything. My ounce of leverage forced him to give me all the money that was in the two pensions (six thousand dollars) in exchange for the house. I couldn't wait to get out of there and escape into Avery's playground. I desperately needed to linger in his laughter and let his smile melt my anger away.

When I picked him up from school, he showed

me the happy faces he had earned. I took him to a frozen yogurt shop to reward him for his good behavior. I modified old habits from my childhood somewhat. Some patterns in our family were worth repeating, like when Father rewarded our performance for participating in a skit in front of the congregation at the kingdom hall. After the meeting, he would stop off at an ice cream parlor and treat us all to a sundae or cone while he sipped on a milkshake. (Perhaps I would've been better off following in Father's footsteps just once, by becoming addicted to milkshakes instead of assholes.)

After his tummy was satisfied, it didn't take much to convince him to go to a park nearby. While driving there, I heard our love theme, "I Can't Smile Without You" playing on the radio. So I serenaded him loudly and obnoxiously. The back of his head barely touched the top of the seat. I looked over in his direction and laughed in between the lyrics. He returned the gleam through a pair of my sunglasses, which buried his brow and struggled to stay on the ridge of his nose. He put his hand up to his head, sighed, and nodded mildly in disbelief at my goofiness. I rested my hand in his lap, and he traced my lifelines.

A few moments later, I heard humming that sounded like it was coming from the backseat. But when I turned down the volume, it stopped. I looked in the rearview mirror. The image of my little girl took me by surprise, for it had been months since she had made an appearance. Her return comforted me. I was afraid that the big bad wolf and dragon had scared her off for good.

Avery noticed the small showers of joy that had suddenly sprung up in my eyes. "Why are you sad?"

"I'm not sad," I said. "I'm just glad that you're here

with me."

As soon as I parked the car, he made a beeline for the swings, and *she* followed him. I pushed him a dozen times and he screamed, "Wee! Push me higher." Each time he made his ascent, his legs of licorice extended outward. And each time he made his descent, his stomach fell to his feet. "Yikes!" he wailed.

"Does your tummy tickle, honey bun?" I asked.

"Yep," he said. He laughed and uttered, "Oh, god, here it comes again!"

My arms were getting restless, and I wanted to float among the bubble gum clouds, too. I settled into the swing next to him. When the wind whispered in my ears, the flavor of freedom was sweet. It didn't take long before I lost myself in a Peter Pan free flight. I heard faint giggling. I glanced over and noticed that she had joined us. When she extended and flexed her legs, her skirt puffed out with the breeze. I heard her whisper, as if she was right next to my cheek, "It's time to let Arthur go." It was the first time I thought that I heard my little girl's voice (outside of her laughter), which seemed to be sweetened by heaven.

"Let's go on the monkey bars," Avery said. His sneakers hit the dirt, and I chased after him, looking back a couple of times to make sure that she was following us.

He climbed ruggedly up on the monkey bars and pleaded with me to join him. But my unsteadiness kept me as a spectator to his boyish charms and fearless fumbles. When he got to the top, he sat down on the slide.

"Okay, honey bun, you can go on the slide a few times, but then we have to go," I said.

"Oh!" he whimpered. I stood at the bottom of the

slide, and he slid down the slippery steel and into my arms.

As Avery climbed up the ladder to make his descent again, she appeared at the top of the slide. She looked down at me. Her lips parted with a shout that only I could hear. "I'm here for you." Then she made her way down through the dark tunnel. The next twenty seconds suspended me in time by the heaviness in my heart. Her little body was like a caterpillar making its way out of its cocoon. Her smile illuminated the black cloud that was hovering over me, and her giggles echoed. As she whirled inside the mysterious cave, she gasped for air, then inhaled all the black cells from my body. Then her baby's breath filled my lungs, which were suffocating from heartbreak. When I reached for her, the embrace was empty and my weariness returned quickly. As I started to walk away, she said, "Don't give up." She held out her arms, and wings of protection suddenly spread behind her. Her free spirit carried her lightly among the sails of the wind. When I watched her image drift slowly away, I became spent.

16

Welcome to the road less traveled.

I was working the swing shift when a security dispatcher alerted me to an apparent robbery that was in progress. An uneasy shiver overcame me, and I asked for the address to be repeated. Although I had never been called there previously and I didn't know the owner, my hands trembled mildly. Suddenly, an overwhelming need to rescue and protect its occupant from ensuing harm sent my patrol car careening corners on two wheels and dodging road kill.

From afar, when I approached the home on the hill, a feeling of familiarity overtook me. One of the entry doors was open, leading me to believe that the intruder had already fled the scene. As I crossed the threshold, my heart fluttered with every breathless beat. The scent of perfume became my intoxicating sedative and steadied the reckless rhythm inside my chest. The fragrance led me into a softly lit parlor, as if to invite, *Enter my beloved temple.* When I saw her, my fears gave way to yearning.

I was mesmerized by her alluring stance. The sheer black cape she wore teased my eyes, allowing me only to catch a glimpse of her sensual silhouette. Rose petals began to fall lightly over her, sprinkling her in passion's dust, and she began to swirl. Upon the first twirl, as the fabric tantalized her breasts with a gentle grazing, her nipples danced to an erection. With each twirl that followed, she revealed more of her mother-of-pearl skin. The glass doors behind her were open, permitting the midnight breeze to pass over the shimmering surface of the swimming pool. While she seduced me with her graceful sashays, the illusion that she was waltzing on water made me wet with wonder. When I approached her, she stopped and extended her hand. Then she stated, "I have come to teach you to fear the darkness no more." When I reached out to take hold of her open hand, she playfully teased, "I know how you like to play hide-and-seek. Come and get me." The lights went out. With the gleam in her eyes being the only illumination, we proceeded to play cat and mouse.

When I found her, I laid her upon a bed of white lilies. Her skin was so soft and her touch so delicate that I couldn't tell if it was the petals I was caressing or her. My nose nestled up the nape of her neck, inhaling her as if she was the incense of ecstasy. The heat permeating from her well of desire ignited my animal endorphins. On the way down my tongue outlined the graceful arch of her shoulders, pausing briefly and ever so lightly across her breasts. As I made my way back up, my lips took in the moisture of her skin, which was growing warmer.

When I found her lips, I nibbled my way around for her feverish tongue. There I lingered like a suckling babe. I allowed her hands to guide me down to where a heat wave was stirring, but not before I had a second helping of her bountiful breasts. My fingers clinched the tip of her nipples, and my tongue painted her ducts with firm and quickened strokes. When her back arched, awaiting to take in my talented tongue, I softly outlined the exterior walls of her pleasure chest with long strokes. When I made my way into the interior walls of her love nest, my strokes became feather-like and my mouth drew her in deeper. Her flesh had swollen into a fountain of pleasure, and she embraced one pinnacle of passion after another.

When I realized that it was music playing and not high notes of her praise for a job well-done, I reached for the snooze button on my clock radio. I became cognizant that I was laying in my bed holding my pillow and not Mrs. Jones. The stunning beauty came to me like a thief in the night, inhabiting my dream state and stealing my heart. It was time to get up and dress for our interlude. I slipped into my toilet technician and dishwashing diva attire and headed off to her house as her cleaning girl—not as her lover.

It looks like my salacious appetite had turned slightly incestuous, as I had fallen for the likes of an older woman. Though she was breathtaking and my initial attraction was physical, the subliminal cravings I had were maternal. Once again, I had fallen into need—not into love—because I expected her to step into my mother's shoes and fix what Father broke. I set out to capture her heart. However, her spirit ended up captivating me, for all the qualities that I found appealing in her were ones that I wished were innate in me. Although my fantasies never materialized into an affair and my soul was still athirst for love's potion, they aroused a curiosity in me which sent me into no-man's-land for a while.

Due to being a glutton for punishment during the pig fest years, I was sick over casting my pearls to swine and suffering from trichinosis. But when my incubation period ended, I was still starving for love. Yet once I discovered that I continued to be a magnet for attracting the same type of harmful bacteria, with the main distinction being primarily in the genitals,

I lost my appetite completely. My anger toward both sexes began to marinate, and a rather malicious stew was brewing. I wanted to settle scores, especially where Arthur was concerned. I was tired of turning the other cheek, only to have him slap me repeatedly.

The first slap came when he knew that my allergies had escalated into asthma while we were still living together, and he still refused to get rid of the cat (Sheba). Then while we were separated but not yet divorced, I went over to our house one day to pick up some old mail. I didn't see Sheba, and I noticed that the litter box, her feeding dishes, and toys were gone. He had given her to a coworker. He complained that it was too much trouble trying to keep the house clean while the house was on the market, because he had to vacuum her hair off the floors every other day.

The second slap came when he failed to accept any responsibility for our troubled marriage. Initially, he refused my request to seek marriage counseling. Then during a very brief trial reconciliation period when I lived with Jay, he begged me to go to counseling with him, only so that he could deny his abusive behavior in our two sessions. I came away from the sessions feeling as though his intentions were to make a fool of me and have the validity of my claims appear absurd. *After all, I was the one who didn't have all my ducks in a row, not him.*

By the time the third slap hit me, we were already divorced. We were victims in a class-action lawsuit against two manufacturers. One suit had to do with the wood siding on our house, and the other dealt with faulty plumbing. Because I had already signed the previous documents as one of the homeowners, my signature was required for the final judgment settlement on the plumbing lawsuit. I assumed that even though I had quitclaimed the deed of our house over to him in the divorce settlement, he was going to be a gentleman and offer me some percentage of the five thousand dollars that he was going to receive for his pain and suffering alone. *But how could I expect a real man to emerge out of a greedy ogre?* Though he knew my struggling circumstance, he offered me nothing. In fact, months before, he had buffaloed me into re-financing our house so that he would have lower mortgage payments. He intimidated me into believing that if he foreclosed, my credit would also go bad. He complained that the three hundred dollars a month his mother was giving him to meet his budget since I left wasn't enough. I realized his game. He had been playing me for months, by trying to remain friends after our divorce, so that he could continue to exploit me in my defeated position. Not only did his actions define him and prove that he belonged to a colony of creatures from the lowest essence, but it became the last straw for me. I refused to see him or return his calls thereafter. Nonetheless, his karma continued to kick me further on down the road.

I was visiting Sophie one day when her youngest son, David, stopped by. He and Arthur worked for the same government municipality. He showed me the announcement in their monthly newsletter. It stated that Arthur had remarried. His bride was a recent college graduate, majoring in psychology. Following a formal ceremony and reception, the lovebirds were off on a honeymoon cruise. The announcement also mentioned his latest promotion.

I responded, "Funny, I could've sworn I already gave him a promotion as a pilot in my novel."

David asked, "He doesn't know how to fly?"

185

"Are you kidding? He couldn't fly himself off an anthill," I said.

David laughed, then continued, "I'm so sorry that I ever helped that prick get his foot in the door there. He walks around strutting like some peacock while he kicked you into a gutter."

"Too bad for his latest victim," I said. "Maybe this time, after he's done playing ring around the rosary, she'll clean his clock."

"How old is she?" Sophie asked.

"She looks like she's in her early twenties," David answered.

"I see a pattern here," I said.

"Which is?" David asked.

"As he goes along, he picks his victims younger and more naive," I said. "I wonder if the next one will even be old enough to drive without a restricted license."

We all laughed, then Sophie said, "That's so he can control them. But not to worry, my dear, because he's going to give her quite an education. Now that she's got someone with a case history like his on her hands, she won't have to do much research for her thesis."

We all laughed again and I added, "Only if she survives his lessons in cruelty."

"I wonder what kind of snow job he did on her," David said.

"I always said he was in the wrong business," I said. "He's a natural when it comes to acting."

"All the charm and ass kissing isn't going to save him when karma comes knocking," David concluded.

17

After the dust settled from my divorce, I was regaining consciousness from my psychological coma and slowly returning to the independent woman that I was before I got married. I moved out of Jay's house and into a one-bedroom apartment. Though I suffered some tremendous losses and essentially had to start over, one of the things I had in my favor was my age. Although it took me twice as long to accomplish a physical task, my mind was fresh with ideas on building another career for myself. I researched the areas of interest to me. I had successfully completed twelve credits and even made the dean's list.

I was in the midst of my second semester, carrying nine credits, when I caught the flu. I was laid up for two weeks, trying to recover from a bad bout of sinusitis. Unfortunately, this brought me back into the twilight zone and my vestibular system was under attack. How quickly I had forgotten what it felt like to be caught in the vicious spin cycle. I was like a hostage who was being held up in my own apartment, unable to go anywhere except to the couch or bed. It reminded me of the days when misery was my constant companion. Soon, I was falling behind in my classes and worried about getting behind in my bills, because if I didn't work I didn't get paid. Regrettably, I allowed fear to take over. I filed for a withdrawal in my classes so that my grade-point average wouldn't drop, and I began to reassess my situation.

The dilemma I was facing was that I didn't have the funds to support myself for an extended period of time while going back to school. Though I had a technical degree, a lot of the credits weren't transferable. In large part, I felt that I was forced to take the easy way out; any degree was better than no degree. *All because Father did me such a grand favor*, by allowing me to stay in school and earn my high school diploma through a work program. However, the work program at that time didn't offer the core classes that are prerequisites for a large number of college courses, which meant that depending on the curriculum that I chose I had to do some serious backtracking. I lacked the physical stamina that I had in previous years when I worked full time and attended night school. And I couldn't give up the cleaning because I needed it to survive.

After talking to a guidance counselor at a community college, I learned that I wasn't eligible for a grant. And even though they didn't offer a disability scholarship, a university in my area did. The scholarship was only applicable toward the last two years of a four-year program. Consequently, I would be required to take all the prerequisites and complete my associate degree at a community college. I would also have to carry twelve credits during each semester and maintain at least a C average. I was frustrated, but I didn't give up hope.

My psychotherapist at the time told me about a private organization that aids displaced individuals in getting the training or education necessary to secure employment. I was convinced that this was the solution to my problem. Perhaps they could provide funding for the remaining credits that I needed toward earning an associate degree. Then I could apply for the disability scholarship at the university. After the clerk reviewed my forms, he said, "I see you're divorced. Do you receive any alimony?"

"Not a penny."

"Do you have any children?" he asked.

"No."

"It's unfortunate, but in order to meet our eligibility requirements, you'd have to be making a little less than what disability pays you."

"I guess I'm getting punished for being responsible," I said. "I don't want to have any children until I know I can take care of them."

"I'm sorry we couldn't help you. You might want to check with some other organizations . . . good luck."

"Could you spare some?" I asked, as I saw the door of darkness and oppression reopen.

So between having to work part time to pay for my tuition and battle my remaining symptoms, I calculated that it would take me twice as long to finish a program that offered a degree. I knew that I had the strength to keep up the hectic pace for a year or two. But I also knew beyond a shadow of a doubt that there was no way that I was going to be able to sustain the pace for six to eight years. This realization discouraged me further. I wanted out of my impoverished situation so badly, yet I did not want to give up my independent lifestyle. I knocked on destiny's door and went searching for an answer.

I concentrated on what I thought I was good at, something that I could do at home in my leisure, requiring minimum financial resources. After receiving positive feedback from the same therapist (regarding the talent she saw during a healing exercise, when I composed unsent letters to my abusers), I made a decision to resurrect my greatest childhood coping mechanism. I quickly enrolled in a nonfiction writing correspondence course. Halfway through the course, one of the assignments was to prepare a short article and query letter. Once the final revisions were made, I submitted the article to several magazines. So when I came home each afternoon, exhausted from cleaning the crap off other people's toilet seats, I would eagerly walk to my mailbox, hoping for an encouraging word from an editor that would validate my efforts. Yet every self-addressed stamped envelope that I opened held a rejection letter. I was coming to the conclusion that I had made another wrong choice. I told myself that if I didn't get an article or poem published by the end of the course, I was going to change directions.

Then one night, as the blazing sun was setting in the west, penetrating the hungry womb of the Gulf, I sat on the eastern shore, watching the ocean's horizon give birth to a full moon. Following a few moments of meditation, I reminded myself and God of the day when I felt the presence of evil trying to devour me. Then I reminded both of us about the vow that I made to help others. Once again, I took off the chasma that was dangling from a chain around my neck. I held it while asking in earnest that I be given a sign—no matter how small—that I was on the right path toward discovering my divine purpose. When I returned home, there was a message on the answering machine from a magazine editor in California. She was interested in publishing my article about eating disorders. My somber mood of confusion shifted to one of fervent certainty. I shouted and jumped around my apartment like a little child, "Thank you! Thank you!"

Although I didn't receive any monetary compensation, I was published a few months later. I continued to pursue the nonfiction market and soon was under contract for a second article. I skipped my way along the yellow brick road, oblivious that it was paved with countless rejections.

As the months passed and I honed my talent, my enthusiasm toward the nonfiction market waned. I lacked the patience and ability to swiftly rebound following each round of rejection letters. I had every confidence that I was headed in the right direction. But I was beginning to feel that perhaps I got off on the wrong exit. Because I didn't have a Ph.D. behind my name and there were so many other authors in the nonfiction market that did, I deduced that expecting any great success on that road was futile. So I went on to explore the avenue of fiction. In view of the fact that I thought I had been dealt a wicked hand in life and was alive to talk about it, I presumed that I was entitled to a life of grandeur. On top of this, I was constantly surrounded with people whom I saw enjoying a grandiose existence. No, I'm afraid that having just learned to crawl was not satisfying enough for my ego. It wanted to be in the race running. I followed my intuition, and after reading a few books on the subject, I set out to write my first novel.

Six months later, the first draft was complete. In efforts to solicit an agent, I spent the next few months sending out queries, which were accompanied by an outline. It didn't take long for me to understand that if I wanted to get an agent or find a publisher, I had to go where they congregate. So in the spring of 1998, I attended the International Women's Writing Guild Conference in Manhattan. I managed to pique the interest of four agents who requested the first three chapters of my novel for their review. A month later, two of the agents politely dismissed my material. The other two (or I should say their underpaid and overworked interns) liked the first three chapters and requested to review the entire novel. Though both agencies ended up rejecting it and didn't elaborate on their decision, their interest encouraged me to persist. For the next five months, I did revision after revision, preparing it for the annual Maui Writers Conference. I temporarily took on extra cleaning jobs so that I would have the funds to attend the event on Labor Day weekend.

The Maui conference differed from the New York conference vastly. The New York conference had only six agents to choose from, of whom I was allowed one to two minutes to verbally pitch my story. (No written material was allowed to be presented.) At the Maui conference, there were over fifty agents to choose from. And as long as I could afford the thirty-dollar fee for each individual session, I was given ten minutes to verbally pitch and/or present written material to the agents in my genre.

Prior to my attending the Maui conference, I entered the outline, my bio, and first page of the novel into *The Manuscript Marketplace*, which is affiliated with the conference. Within weeks, I was notified through the mail that a few book agents and an agent from Mutual Film Company were interested. I was perplexed because I had written a novel—not a screenplay. I thought it might have been a ploy to ensure my attendance since I had been warned that the traveling expenses alone were going to be exorbitant. Thus, it wasn't until I got there and saw the agent's name listed in the itinerary as one of the speakers that I started to believe it was true and not just a moneymaking venture. Then, once I sat down with her and she reviewed my material, I received further validation. She told me that she would be interested in seeing my novel adapted into a screenplay. I imagine that my lack of confidence was probably plastered across my face when I replied, "I've read a few books on screen-writing and recently purchased a software program for my computer. But I've never written a screenplay."

"This story would make a good movie for some network like Lifetime," she encouraged. "And you seem to be a natural when it comes to dialogue. If it gets picked up by one of the networks, it will get rewritten anyway. So what have you got to lose?"

Because of my track record and all the years I was conditioned into having a pessimistic outlook, I needed a second person to validate her confidence in my ability. So the following day, I met with another agent who worked for ABC. He was honest, telling me that he worked in the area of comedy and sitcoms and not in drama. But he gave me the courtesy of looking over my material. "This could be a great story for the *Movie of the Week*," he said. "I really like your dialogue. . . . I told you before, I don't work in this area, but if you send me a treatment, I'll pass it along to the right people."

What I found odd about this was that I had already been exploring the screenwriting angle long before I entered the *Manuscript Marketplace*. This was based on the suggestions from a couple of agents that I had previously submitted my story to through the mail. Even though I saw evidence that my intuition was steering me in the proper direction, I was still skeptical, thinking that possibly the agents were just being polite. That is when I received my third confirmation.

During some of the intermission periods, I had been keeping company with a gentleman and his father. On the last and final day, the father was there without his son. When I asked where his son was, the father mentioned that he was too depressed to attend. His son had been soliciting his story diligently for the past three days but couldn't find one agent who was interested in it. I felt sad for his son and slightly guilty, because by the time the conference was over I had two interested parties from the screenplay angle and five who were interested from the book angle. At last, I found something tangible that could explain a purpose to all the suffering I had endured throughout my life.

When I returned home, I didn't waste any time attempting to adapt the story into a screenplay. However, as the next few weeks slipped away, so did my zeal, for every week brought another rejection from a book agent. I dwelled on how much time and effort I had put into the novel; how many social invitations from friends and relatives I had turned down because I wanted to complete another chapter; and how many hours I spent staying up until 3 *a.m.* to write and then rise at 7 *a.m.* to get ready for work. I imagined how I would feel if I were to expend all my energies into writing the script, and at the end have it be rejected, or worse, have someone who had the connections initially reject it but then rewrite it and sell it themselves. Layered within this insecurity was my fear—not only of failure—but of success. So after I received the last rejection from a book agent, I fell deeply into despair, allowing the demons of depression to almost cripple me completely. With every passing day that I didn't work on the script, I grew more anxious. As I completely lost my appetite, my weight dropped and I had difficulty sleeping. I had an intense amount of nervous energy. When I wasn't physically working, the only thing I could do was pace around my apartment. I felt like a hamster on a wheel. I knew that if I didn't snap out of it soon, I was going to wind up in a psychiatric facility.

I attributed the gloom, fatigue, and having a difficult time concentrating to dropping the ball on the opportunity of a lifetime. Being labeled as disabled made me feel like a convict with a criminal record. I was tired of serving a life sentence for a crime I didn't commit. So once more, I searched for a security blanket. I set out to find a profession that wouldn't take me long to get educated in, something that I could part time, earn a decent income in, and still pursue my dream. That's when, in February 1999, I took a similar path down the healing highway when I enrolled in a massage therapy program.

The foremost desire to become a massage therapist was born out of the simple solace I felt from experiencing touch. Between Father's abandonment, Mom's absence, and the rest of my family divided, I often felt like I was in solitary confinement. Moreover, the craft of writing can be extremely isolating. So whenever I could afford it, I went to a nearby massage and beauty school to get a massage at a discount rate. On my more creative days, listening to ethereal music while I was getting massaged elicited ideas or poetic phrases that I used in my writing. In moments of melancholy, I wept silently while the student massaged my blues away. This helped me discover, firsthand, a new resource to help heal myself and possibly others.

Consequently, I set my sights on a new goal: becoming a licensed aesthetician and massage therapist so that I could obtain employment in a spa setting. In case massage was too physically taxing on me, having two licenses was the assurance that would prevent me from winding up on the system again.

When I signed up for the fourteen-month program and gave the school a substantial down payment, I didn't reveal my disability. I assumed that doing so would give them a reason to refuse me on the basis of insurance liability reasons. The tuition for the two programs was approximately ten thousand dollars. I didn't want to exhaust the bulk of the money in the investment accounts that I had started after my divorce. That's when things got tricky. The week before my classes started, I finally came clean with the financing director. She reassured me that I wouldn't have any problems if I applied for a school loan—this despite the fact that my previous school loan for the architectural program that I was in years earlier was revoked halfway through the repayment term because of my disability status. So I filled out the request forms and began the routine of going to school four nights a week and most of the day on Saturdays. In order to meet the schedule and physically demanding portion of the program, I scaled back on my cleaning jobs and only worked three, half days a week. (While one hour each night in class was spent practicing on a student or the public, two hours were designated for a lecture.)

In late April, I received papers from Social Security informing me that my case was up for medical review. I didn't have any reservations about passing and getting approved for another three years, especially when there hadn't been any change in my condition since the previous review. The only difference was that I was being treated for depression and being prescribed an antidepressant. My only concern was a question inquiring whether I was in school. In view of the fact that I had applied for a school loan, I thought that if I answered "no" and they found out that I wasn't telling the truth, I could get into serious trouble.

I expressed my awareness of their returning-to-work policy and the trial work period I was entitled to.

According to their guidelines, I was allowed to earn any amount of money for up to nine months. (The months don't have to be consecutive and can be stretched out over sixty months.) And grossing over two hundred dollars a month counted as a trial work month. Once I completed nine of these, my case would be reviewed. Then I would be given three months of severance pay, and my Medicare coverage would continue for thirty-nine months. If there were any months that my income grossed less than five hundred dollars over the three years that followed, my benefits would automatically be reinstated for that month. I mailed the form, confident that they would be happy to see that I had taken the initiative to get off the system without being told to do so.

While I was waiting for Social Security's decision, the financing director at the school informed me that there was a problem in the school loan application process. The Florida Department of Education didn't want to give me a loan because of my disability status. She was trying to persuade them to reconsider on the grounds that I would present them with a letter from my physician stating that my condition had improved enough for me to pursue gainful employment as a masseuse. She told me to stay in school, assuring me that she would try another source if they turned me down again. My doctor didn't hesitate to compose a letter on my behalf.

Returning to school gave me a sense of pride again. I was more determined than ever to turn my life around, not just in the area of employment but also in where I was living. When Arthur and I finally broke all lines of communication and he set his sights on a new victim, I asked him to inform me if and when he decided to put our house back on the market to sell it.

My intuition was at play again. I was cleaning a customer's home one day (who was also a real estate agent) when I learned that there was a sales contract pending on the house. Though I knew that I wasn't going to get any proceeds from the sale, eliminating the mortgage made me eligible to buy something of my own again.

Within a month, I found a one-bedroom condo that I liked and was within my budget. For nonincome verification purposes, I was required to put twenty percent down. I easily liquidated ten percent out of a mutual fund to secure the sale. I've always maintained excellent credit. But my creditors taught me early on in my disability that honesty isn't always the best policy. I might as well have had a criminal record because they treated me like one by denying me credit. It wasn't until I learned to stretch the truth and say that I had a cleaning business that I was able to get any credit cards or a car loan. So trying to work around this technicality in the home loan application process came as no surprise.

Just days after I signed the buyer's agreement and scheduled the closing for the middle of July, I received a letter from Social Security. Before they received all the medical information from my doctor, they had already transferred my file over to the Disability Determinations Division. They claimed that they didn't have enough information in my file, so they were sending me to *their* doctors. I sensed trouble, but I cooperated anyway. Additionally, the Florida Department of Education sent me a letter claiming that they never received the letter from my doctor. I knew they were lying, for I, as well as the finance director, had mailed them a copy. Thus, they used this excuse to deny my request for a loan again. I refused to drop out of school, knowing that I was still responsible for half the tuition if I did. I reasoned, at worst, I wouldn't take the skin care program, and I would put the remainder of the tuition for the massage program on my credit cards.

In efforts to distract myself and to remain positive, I turned my focus toward the excitement of being a homeowner again. However, when I went to liquidate the remaining ten percent that was necessary to purchase the condo and cover closing costs, I was told that the company was merging with another and that the liquidation process would take thirty business days. I had no choice but to delay the closing date accordingly. A couple of weeks later, I was watching the local news when I learned that the unimaginable had happened. An FBI investigation revealed that the fund managers were being indicted for fraud, and that any of the remaining monies that weren't pissed away on lavish lifestyles were being held in escrow. It was imminent that the case was going to end in bankruptcy court. There was little chance that I (and more than five thousand other victims in South Florida) would recoup any of the original investment. And if I did, it was probably going to be pennies on the dollar and years away. Once more, a dark cloud was looming on my potential joy and sense of purposefulness that a new career and residence could offer.

I was waiting for the next shoe to drop, for the bank to tell me that I had been turned down for a mortgage because Arthur's plans to sell the house had fallen through. The negative feelings multiplied when I called our old telephone number and discovered that it was still in service and hadn't changed. When I finally contacted him at work, he apologized for not telling me about the sale. He went on to gloat that he sold the house for over one hundred thousand dollars. He and his new wife were tenants to the new homebuyers until the construction on their new townhouse was finished. He was curious as to why I wanted to know about the house. When I told him that I was hoping to buy a condo (which was over twenty years old), I elaborated on being denied a school loan and the money I lost in the fund. I did my best not to whine or lose my cool. I quickly did the numbers in my head, remembering the refinancing documents I had signed a few years back, calculating that he probably made a twenty-thousand-dollar profit. Though I had enormous contempt for him after our divorce, a part of me logically rationalized his selfishness. After all, when we were going through our divorce, he wasn't in a position to pay me back the money that I used toward the down payment and closing costs on our home. But now, five years later, he was in a position to pay me back. Since his life was on the upswing, I was looking for some shred of decency in him, that he would extend some courtesy and offer me any help. He showed me the kind of marauder he always was by his response. "I'm sorry to hear that."

Just when I had come to the conclusion that the bad guys always win, some good news knocked on my door. A classmate told me about a state-funded vocational rehabilitation program. I wanted to kick myself for allowing my past negative experiences with other agencies to keep from exploring this avenue sooner. I immediately sought their assistance. Though they couldn't pay for what had already been done academically, they agreed to pay a portion of the remaining tuition for the massage and skin care program.

So there I was, scrambling to find a way to purchase

the condo, looking at it as my reward for not giving up. In light of the fact that I had excellent credit, the credit card companies had been offering me low interest rates during the past year. I guesstimated that if I were to take out cash advances against my credit cards to close the deal, this wouldn't be reflected on my credit report for six weeks. And I was praying that the lender wouldn't do a last-minute credit check and refuse to approve me on the basis of my debt ratio being too high. My real estate agent knew the predicament I was in and asked if I had any family member who could present a gift letter to the lender on my behalf. Though Jay, who had been living in another state by then, offered to liquidate a portion of his retirement account to loan me the money, I didn't want him to suffer any early withdrawal penalties because I had made another bad choice. Consequently, I wired him the funds, and he deposited them into his account. He sent back a gift letter, along with proof that the funds came out of his account. I didn't seriously calculate the minimum that I would be required to pay each month on my credit card accounts. My main objective was getting into the condo and buying time. I reasoned that by the time I closed on the condo, I would be only weeks away from finishing the massage program. If I passed the finals, then within four to six weeks after that I could take the national board exam. If I passed it, I could be working as a therapist by the end of October or the beginning of November.

It was mid-September when I moved into my condo. I was delighted that the closing went through without any more snags. I was proud of my re-sourcefulness and my ability to maintain an A average in my studies through all the upheaval. Most of my classmates passed their school final the first time.

So I wasn't concerned or surprised when I passed mine. However, the national board exam was a different matter. There were a number of students who had taken the exam twice and failed both times. I scheduled my exam date and tried to stay positive. Yet fate had different plans for me.

In early October, I received another letter from Social Security. They informed me that they had made a decision to terminate my benefits in December. They stated that I could hire an attorney to appeal their decision, and my benefits would continue during this process (which could take about six months). But if I lost the appeal, all the benefits that I received during that time would have to be paid back. Drained of all my financial resources, I went to the Legal Aid office. There I learned that the benefits that I had been receiving, and the ones that were going to be terminated, were about one thousand dollars over the annual income limit. (They base their decision on the previous year's income, not on someone's current situation.) So I wasn't eligible to receive their assistance.

I was disgusted by the fact that crime suspects who are taken into police custody have more rights than I did. If they can't afford an attorney, they are appointed one free of charge. Then, if they are convicted and sent to prison, they are entitled to earn a college degree through the *criminal scholarship* fund. I was coming to the cynical conclusion that in some cases crime does pay.

This disheartening discovery resurrected the losses I experienced when I got divorced. Again, I was stripped of the armor that was necessary if I wanted a fighting chance. Without my benefits and with no license to secure employment, my back was up against the wall. And the small amount that I was earning through my cleaning jobs wasn't even close to meeting my basic living expenses.

I had kept all the documents to prove and plead my case. On the one hand, I had been denied a school loan based solely upon my disability status; on the other, my benefits were being terminated based on the premise that I was no longer disabled. To substantiate the injustice further, I had been reviewed and renewed by Social Security three years earlier and nothing in my condition had changed since then. With this, I contacted the American Civil Liberties Union and the U.S. Department of Justice Disability Rights Division. After a few weeks both agencies denied me any assistance, claiming that it was out of their jurisdiction. Every door of hope was closing in on me. I was completely despondent, convinced that I was bound to remain a slave at being a victim.

On the psychological level, I thought that I was doing everything in my power to get me out of the defeated position I had been stuck in for the past several years. I knew that it had to start with a new blueprint to rebuild my self-esteem. The solid foundation—I thought—was getting reeducated in another field. And owning my own home again would give me security. But every step I was taking toward that end was followed by another enormous mountain of adversity to climb. I lived in the greatest country in the world—America, "land of the free and home of the brave." I was brave but far from being free, especially when it came to the pressure that I felt in my responsibility to live the American dream. Everyone else was entitled to those opportunities except me. And although I was not gorgeous, lady luck did smile on me attractively. Yet I could not use my looks to my advantage while being plagued with such hideous problems?

On the emotional level, that old familiar feeling of everyone else being in control of my life found its insidious way back to me. Each setback I had encountered only reinforced feelings of unworthiness and hopelessness. Here I was again thrown into the black abyss, with my only friend being my survival instinct; and now even this was being threatened. Additionally, the greatest talent that I possessed (writing) is one of the toughest professions going. And it forced me to come face to face with the biggest issue in my life (rejection) repeatedly. Indeed, I was so full of venom that nothing could stop my poisonous pen from bringing those who wronged me to justice.

Astrologically speaking, I thought that being born under the zodiac sign of Capricorn was another cruel joke that the universe had played on me. Two aspects that are important to Capricorns are career and status. I had no career, and every attempt I made to create one was blown out of the water. Where status was concerned, fate was determined to prove that I was just another one of society's ills. The other aspect that's vital to Capricorns is the need for stability and security. Well, my security and stability were rocked right out the cradle the day Mom died.

Finally, on the spiritual level, I was convinced that the universe was against me. There was no way to change my doomed destiny. God had deserted me, and cursing him was becoming a habit. The recent teases were just another way that I was being used as a punching bag. The only thing that was keeping me alive was my anger. It tossed me into the *I'm not going to let those bastards win* tornado. My mirror of great expectations, which fueled my ambition to succeed when I was younger, was now reflecting devastating disappointments. I was totally disillusioned with life, people, and the system. I was shaken to the core. Through all my tribulations and beyond all my shattered dreams, I finally crumbled.

I went to confront my Creator and drown in the belly of the sea. In the early years of my life, oars of strength enabled me to row with courage against some of the most unforgiving currents. When I lost both of these (Mom and Nana), I continued to battle the raging waters. Then when my vessel capsized, I treaded the tumultuous tides alone. Finally, after everything had been stripped from me, I tumbled. Tossed and thrown about, my perilous journey left me battered by the tempestuous sea of life, all washed up, and on a shore of regrets.

My heart was overflowing with hatred. My sadness painted the seashore. My tears left me drowning in puddles of Father's sinful abandonment. The angry boils of injustice inflicted upon me submerged me deeper into despair. I was beginning to relate to Job.

With dusk off at a momentary distance, the beach was silent except for the sound of the surf, the call of the wild, and heaven's entreaty. I walked until my legs could carry me no more. Then I fell to my feet, crying out, "What the hell do you want from me, God? How much more do you think I can take?"

I was sinking into spiritual quicksand. My secret death wish caught up with me at last. The demons were dancing in all their wickedness, assuming that I was down for the count. They rubbed their claws together, chanting, "Finally she's ours. She's so bitter from all the pain that we seasoned her soul with. We never cared for sweets. It was worth the wait." They were waiting for me to take the final plunge so that they could carry me off into eternal misery. The angels encircled me in their glory, the weight of their wings doing their best to keep the demons down.

My sobs of isolation made me collapse into a deep slumber. In my dream state, the many ghosts of the children who lost their battle at the hands of their abusive killers came alive again. Their voices awoke the child inside of me who had been resting in heavenly peace. Then all the ghosts, of the women who lost their lives behind the fists of their assassins and whose words were hushed, spoke out, denouncing their birthright of oppression and reclaiming their rights for equality. These joined the children, shouting for justice. Peaches was back. She was commissioned by the pleas from these supporters into the chambers of divine justice.

They were all carrying torches. In combined effort, they turned Peaches's torch, which was barely a flicker, into a giant blazing torch. They handed her a great sword of justice that they all sharpened against a blade of virtue. Peaches led, with the torch in one of her hands and the sword at her side. They headed for the promised-land playground, a playground promised to them but never delivered when they were born into a bad childhood, abandoned, rejected, or violated through acts of hatred. This once-joyous place was destroyed, taken over by evil creatures and scary monsters.

They cheered Peaches on, "No more darkness!" She opened the gates ready to expose and eliminate.

The abusers who liked to kick their victims had their legs extended out, ready to kick her as she approached them. She yelled, "Shiver me timbers!" picked them up one by one by the edge of their heels, flipped them, and sent them spiraling down into a heap of broken bones.

Those men who liked to punch their victims saw her coming, as did those women who liked to use objects to beat their children. They screamed for clemency. "We did the best we could!"

She held no mercy for these wrongdoers as she drew her sword. "Enough excuses! You did know better."

"But we were *saved*."

"That isn't a license to do whatever you want." She chopped their hands off one at a time.

Her supporters cheered again, "No more darkness!" She heard shouts of profanity coming from those who liked to demean others, making them feel worthless with their verbal and mental tactics. She ripped their tongues out, leaving them speechless.

When those men who reveled in intimidating women with their position saw this, they ran for shelter. Her supporters aimed their torches in their direction. They revealed, "Over there Peaches! Go get 'em, and knock 'em dead!"

She found and dethroned all the varmints who had been masquerading as men, claiming to be created in God's image. She smashed their crowns with her sword. She yelled, "You can run, but you'll never hide from justice." Then she handed her torch to her supporters until she was done banging their heads together. Once they were brain damaged, she declared, "A mind is a terrible thing to waste. Think your way out of this one boys."

Her ghostly supporters handed her torch back to her. Then they all joined hands, formed a circle, and galloped in circular motion. She stood in the middle of the enormous circle and began skipping with everlasting joy. She raised her torch up and down in rhythm with their cheers. "Our voices will be silenced no longer! They shall kill us no more! We will shine and prevail over their darkness!"

Now it came to be that, although her heart was in the right place, Peaches was getting to be a little too big for her britches. The sword of Satan was tempting, but it didn't belong in God's court. She needed a reality check, understanding that if she was to take the law into her own hands, she would be no better than her abusers. My divine dream ended after I reconciled my resolve for revenge against my abusers, leaving it up to a power greater than myself.

By the time I finished my spiritual sleepwalk, twilight was on the horizon. A myriad of angels removed the blanket of death that had been smothering me. Then they immediately practiced CPR on me: celestial prophetic restoration. I rubbed my sand-swept eyes, still whispering, "No more darkness." All at once, the thick gray clouds parted, and the raindrops continued to fall everywhere around but upon me no more. The sun burst forth with an almost blinding intensity. With the flick of his finger, the Lord sent the demons spiraling back into their devilish dimension. As I left the darkness and moved into the light, the shackles came off me. The fight was over. The love inside me to help God's children won over the hatred of not being able to forgive myself for letting others take away my power.

Until complete consciousness returned, a voice from above spoke loudly to me so that I wouldn't mistake his voice for any other. *Arise my precious child. All the pain and suffering was to groom you for something greater. How shall my lost children find their way home without someone to guide them? The time has come. You are but one mortal, yet your words will strengthen many. So many tears my children have shed. You are one of many I have chosen to dry their eyes. You must save my children as I have saved you. Such a big job for such a little girl, I know. Fear not and forsake me never, for I am with you always. Take my hand, and I shall be with you every step of the way. You see my precious child, you are never alone. My love is timeless.*

There were two sets of footprints in the sand. I recognized the child's effortless skip and carefree spirit. Peaches was resurrected. She returned stronger, braver, and wiser. The sea breeze made her skirt cling to her legs and then puff out with the gentle ease in her skipping. Her ringlets bounced as she sprung into the air and pounced onto the oncoming waves that were rolling in with the tide. Her impish grin burst into a playful giggle. Her steps meshed into my steps as the warm waters tingled our feet and tickled our toes. She placed her small hand inside mine as I looked down at her with a sense of deep love. She ran ahead of me laughing. A flock of seagulls were in flight above us, and I chased her sun-drenched silhouette down the surf. When I caught up with her, she carried me on the back of her butterfly wings and into the shallow water. As I held onto her tightly, she held her arms open and up toward the sky. We twirled with the ocean air catching our faces in the brilliant sunshine.

So now I was sure. The little girl who had been playing hide-and-seek with me over the past few years wasn't my child. Rather, it was the little girl inside of me who had died the day when my beloved Nana was laid to rest. She had come to wage war on the evil enemies who wanted to destroy the good inside of me, making me just as bitter as they were. She and I stepped up to the front lines together.

Following a couple of days of hysteria, I finally

found someone in the system who was willing to stand up for me. My vocational rehabilitation counselor wrote a letter on my behalf to Social Security, asking them to reinstate my benefits until I completed *all* my training and then passed my boards. She also asked them to consider continuing my benefits through a trial work period. I wouldn't know the outcome of the letter for a few weeks. But this encouraged me to keep going. I prayed hard, trying not to obsess over how I was going to pay the high credit card bills that started coming in. I began revolving my credit, paying off the balance of one with another.

When the beginning of November came, I had two reasons to celebrate. The first one was on behalf of passing the national board exam for massage with flying colors. The second one came in the form of a letter from Social Security. They had sent my file to one of their offices in another county to be reviewed a second time. Thereafter, they came to the decision to reinstate my benefits and grant me a trial work period. By the time the millennium was coming to a close, I had been approved for a second mortgage loan on the condo. I had put twenty percent down on the condo when I bought it, so I had that much in equity to borrow against. With these funds, I paid off most of my credit card debt.

But even with all this good news, I was still struggling with depression, an inability to concentrate, and severe fatigue. My appetite declined sharply, and I had no desire for food at all. I was barely consuming a thousand calories a day, yet I was rapidly packing on the pounds. Then when I started losing more and more of my hair every time I washed or combed it, I knew something was amiss physiologically. I had not had a complete physical in two years. I went to the doctor thinking that the battle I had been through the last several months had taken a toll on me. And I had another disease that was life altering, such as cancer or diabetes. Fortunately, just like all the bomb threats but no actual explosions that I had lived through, it was an ailment that was manageable with medication. When I was diagnosed as having a hypothyroid, not only was I was relieved, but I had a newfound respect for myself as well. I had made it through the worst crisis period of my life despite this new ailment that had been lurking.

As hushes from heaven eased my plight, I finished school and secured a position in a spa. After making it through the series of tests, which eventually made me stronger, the Lord sounded his trumpet. My soul was being called upon to slay my last dragon. The buried and tattered tome of the past was about to be open, and a dirty family secret revealed.

18

I was born a five-pound, twelve-ounce lightweight. But after Mom died, my caretakers couldn't bear to hear me cry, so I often had a bottle in my mouth. Therefore, by the time Helen and Father married, I had grown out of my cuddly baby stage and into a little butterball. Though I was taught early on to stuff my feelings with oral fixations, my growth spurts kept me slim until adolescence arrived. That's when I began to feel awkward and fat, because my breasts weren't growing at the same rate as my curvaceous hips and buttocks.

I was fourteen when my obsession over losing my boyfriend's attention, which I was able to capture since I was in the third grade, sent me to a diet class. I was the youngest one there, so I felt like the odd man out. Tipping the scale at one hundred fifteen pounds made me far from obese. But most of the girls my age were taller, and the ones who were petite like me were ninety-pound dolls. When the facilitator of the group mentioned the binge-and-purge cycle that the Romans from past centuries used to practice, I had been struggling with the program for a few weeks. I took it out of context and began exploring this approach to lose weight. Within two weeks, I was getting compliments about how good I looked, and I was soon turning the head of my old boyfriend again. Practicing the technique on a regular basis gave me the approval and attention that I craved. In the early stages of the disorder, it felt so good gorging on fatty foods that were rich in carbohydrates without having to pay for the indulgence with my appearance. Little did I realize the noose I was putting around my neck and how quickly the daily routine catapulted me into a potentially fatal addiction. Initially, my only fear was that someone would recognize the red abrasions on the knuckles of my right hand, where I had put my finger down my throat to induce vomiting. While grave denial sheltered my psyche, I wasn't aware that Father and Helen had long since groomed me to become another secret agent in their house of lies.

Helen always paid for the groceries every week with a personal check. She usually wrote the check fifty dollars over the actual amount of the bill. This was so that she would have extra spending money. Hence, most of the food choices that she made were lacking in nutritional value. When I was younger, I resented her for this. Whenever I was told to prepare dinner, it often meant separating a pound of ground beef into seven hamburger patties. Or, if chili was on the menu, I had to add an extra can of tomato sauce and kidney beans into the chili to increase the servings. As I grew up, though, and was threatened with the idea of being totally dependent on a selfish man for my subsistence, I sympathized with her situation. When it came to my gluttony, not having our cupboards stocked was a blessing for me. If I had been able to indulge more frequently, my daily habit more than likely would have snowballed into dangerous circumstances.

Furthermore, Helen took advantage of our obligation to pay rent when we turned sixteen, which meant more spending money for her. So between this expense and being responsible for buying my own clothes, gas for my car, and car insurance, I had little money left over to satisfy my voracious vice. Not to mention that having the resources to move out when I was eighteen was a higher priority, especially after the severe beating. That's when I was petrified that Father might catch me in the act and find another excuse to beat me, so I temporarily stopped forcing myself to throw up. But by then my stomach had expanded, and it took larger amounts of food to give me the sensation of being full. As a result, I gained forty pounds in four months. Saying that I felt extremely ugly would be an understatement. At five feet, two inches tall and tipping the scale at almost one hundred sixty pounds, I looked and felt like a beach ball. I made promises to myself and vows to God to keep from returning to my surreptitious lifestyle. But I incessantly fell short of my demands. It was too much work and required the discipline that I didn't have at the time. So when anything bad happened to me, I attributed it to God's punishment for defiling the unblemished body that I was born with.

Father's cloud of control had crept up on me as a young girl. Once I escaped his captivity and the cult's domination, I had no idea that this coping mechanism would chase me into womanhood. During its seven-year reign, I didn't develop anemia, throat blisters from stomach acid, rotten teeth, a ruptured stomach or esophagus, and my menstruation cycle wasn't inter-rupted. It was only after receiving medical treatment for a peptic ulcer and electrolyte imbalance when I was twenty, that I knew I had to stop the vicious binge-and-purge cycle. I was successful and had few urges or relapses, until the silent killer returned to the scene of the crime.

It was shortly after I moved out of Jay's and into my apartment when I received a telephone call from Helen. She told me that Kara was in the hospital and was asking to see me. Helen didn't fill me in on the details. She merely assured me that Kara hadn't been in an accident and was in no physical danger. It wasn't until I got to the hospital that I was directed to the psychiatric ward.

When I entered the room, Helen was there. Kara was dressed in her clothes and sitting on the bed. Helen stayed for a few minutes and then left us alone to talk. "What happened?" I asked.

"Since I've been staying in our old house, I've been having nightmares, like the one I had last night." (Father had converted the house we grew up into a duplex to generate rental income. Kara and her three children lived on one side, while Witnesses from his congregation lived on the other.)

"What is the nightmare about?" I asked.

"Some guy is chasing me," she stammered. "When he catches me, I hit him with a big rock before he can hurt me. I don't remember doing this, but Mother said when I called her it was about two o'clock in the morning. She said that I was talking in a child's voice and I just kept saying, 'Mommy, save me!'"

"Then what happened?"

"I can't remember. Mother said that when she and Dad came over and tried to talk to me, I was out of it and crying and shaking."

"So they brought you here."

"I guess so," she said.

"Did you recognize the guy in the nightmare?" Her face paled, and she started to tremble.

I tugged at her feet. "What is it? You can tell me."

"No I can't," she said. I promised them I wouldn't

215

tell."

"Look . . . I can't help you until you tell me what's bothering you."

She was silent for a few moments, then she whimpered and blurted out, "When we were kids, Jack would take Beth and Kate into his bedroom closet. He made me stand outside the door to make sure that no one was coming; and he forced them to have sex. They cried and begged him to stop, but he just kept doing it." Her cheeks became saturated with tears.

I hugged her for a couple of moments before I asked, "How old were you?"

"I don't know . . . maybe thirteen."

"Did he ever do it to you?"

"No. Just Beth and Kate."

"I can't believe that this was going on and I never even knew about it," I said. I felt guilty that I was living in the house while the incest appeared to be in its early stages. "And what about Mother and Daddy? Did they know?"

"No. Jack threatened to kill us if we ever told anyone. He was so mean to us that we believed him."

"Do they know now?" I asked.

"No. They probably wouldn't believe me," she said, "especially Mother. Her *precious king* never does anything wrong."

"Did you tell anyone here about it?"

"No," she answered.

"You have to. That's what they're here for—to help you. It's the only way you're going to get better."

Her lips were trembling and her hands were shaking. "No! No! Not Kate!" she began to sob loudly. A staff member came in to console her and asked me to wait out in the hall.

Helen was in the hall talking to a psychiatrist.

216

As soon as I revealed the ugly secret to the psychiatrist, Helen acted surprised and concluded, "Don't be too long. Your father's waiting downstairs, and he hasn't seen her yet today. They'll only allow two people at a time in here." Then she disappeared. The psychiatrist asked me a few questions. The only insight I could give her was to tell her that Jay had confessed to me just a few months before that Helen's stepfather had molested him.

When I went downstairs, I saw Father in the waiting area. I looked directly into his eyes with such a disdainful expression that he literally flinched. He tried to hug me, but I brushed him off. Before he went to see Kara, he pulled Helen over into a corner, where they talked softly. When Helen returned and Father disappeared, there were no empty chairs in the waiting area. A man offered Helen his chair. "No thank you," she said. "I'll just sit down here on the floor next to *my daughter*." When I told Helen what Jay had told me, she went into detail about how her stepfather had abused her and her sister when they were children. I was feeling ill and wanted to leave, but she persuaded me to stay until Father returned.

When he returned, all three of us walked out to the parking lot together. Though Helen was acting un-usually friendly toward me, I didn't suspect anything was awry until she invited me to join them for coffee. When I insisted on going home, she invited me to their house for dinner the following evening. I smiled politely, without asking them why their *dead* daughter was suddenly alive again. "I'll call you about tomorrow," I lied.

I knew that our family had its problems and that, in a lot of ways, I had been raised in a very backward fashion. I had always tried my best not to look up at others who had what I didn't. To avoid feeling any more sorry for myself than I already did, a counterfeit calm throughout most of my adulthood enabled me with self-deceptive poise to reassure myself that matters could be worse. I told myself that I may have been brought up in a severely dysfunctional family, but at least sexual abuse wasn't a common denominator. In my wildest dreams, I never imagined that the black plague infecting our family tree was sexual abuse. That kind of conduct went on only in homes where alcoholism or drug abuse was prevalent, not in homes where Bible verses were quoted on a daily basis.

Kara married her childhood sweetheart at eighteen, and they started a family almost immediately. But unfortunately, she and her husband grew apart as he went on to explore, and eventually settle into, a homosexual lifestyle. When he left, he rarely looked back, leaving her to raise his two daughters and son without paying her child support. Kara spent the better part of her youth working tirelessly to support her family. Nevertheless, because she was a high school dropout, the job opportunities were extremely limited. Within a couple of years she remarried, and within the first year she had another daughter. While she continued to work at minimum-wage jobs, her second husband was home helping himself to his two stepdaughters. After he pleaded guilty to molesting them, he was sent to prison. As part of the recovery process, she and her daughters were required to go to counseling regularly for a year. The therapeutic work she was doing with her daughters had stirred up painful memories.

Kara was released after three days and prescribed antianxiety medication. In the meantime, some self-destructive demons came clawing at my door. They were famished and begged me to return to my recid-ivistic ways. I refused to feed them and set out on my criminal investigation to determine why I had the overwhelming urge to purge again.

I telephoned Jack, who was living in another state. To my surprise, he didn't deny the behavior that Kara had accused him of. He felt embarrassment and shame, and as an adult he had previously sought the forgiveness of Beth and Kate. I sensed that he was uncomfortable rehashing this part of his past because he kept trying to change the subject. Finally, I said, "I know this isn't a pleasant topic. I'm not judging you. You were a child yourself when you did those things. My concern is that somehow I might have been abused myself, not by you but someone else."

"What makes you think that?"

"Since I visited Kara in the hospital, I've been having nightmares and the overwhelming desire to return to the bulimia."

"Bulimia—is that where you make yourself throw up?" he asked.

"Yes."

"Do you have any memories of being abused?"

"Not really. I have just one memory that stops right before anything happens. So I can't really accuse this person of anything."

"I understand," he said.

"Jay told me that Helen's stepfather molested him. Did he molest you?"

"No," he answered.

"Someone had to teach you that behavior; other-wise you wouldn't just start doing it to your siblings."

"You're right," he said.

"So who was it?"

He sighed, then said, "I can't tell you, and I really

don't think you want to know."

Even though Helen's face popped into my head. "Was it our cousin, Tom?" I asked.

"Y-e-s. How'd you guess?"

"He's the one I have the memory about, and I keep seeing his eyes," I said.

When I finished our conversation, I did believe that Tom (Father's nephew) may have introduced Jack to the behavior. Or, I may have offered him a scapegoat. In any case, I was intuiting that there was more than one child rapist on the loose. I recalled all the times that I saw Helen frequent Jack's room shortly after he had earned his privilege as a teenage boy and got his own room. I never questioned their late-night talks verbally or internally, for I was serving the needs of a different master, becoming a slave to my addiction. Then my mind drifted back to all the pitchers of beer that she encouraged him to share with her as a minor when Father often treated us to pizza after the meetings. I was imagining what went on with him and Helen behind his bedroom door while he was growing into manhood. All the clothes, guitars, and music lessons that she bought him appeared to be gifts of guilt. For the first time, being an object of Helen's rejection was more appealing than the heartrending truth that Jack had to live with all those years by being a target of her affections.

I momentarily flashed back to the day that I came home from school, which was just weeks after my severe beating, and found Jack holding an ice pack on his face. "What happened?" I asked.

He removed the ice pack and showed me his black eye and lip, which was cut. "I got beat like you, only he took the belt buckle to my face."

"Why?" I asked.

"He said I was making him look bad to the other elders in the congregation. They're thinking about removing him from being an elder."

"So he said it's because of all the trouble you've been getting into lately?" I asked.

"Yep. You better not let him or Mother see us talking. Otherwise, he's going to beat us again."

I felt guilty for all the times I had poked fun at him and Kara, when we were children, because they both had to repeat the second grade over. When I realized how wrong I had been to think Father and Helen had shown favoritism toward them, I also put aside my sibling rivalry. This appalling discovery (sexual abuse) made me realize that they were suffering the consequences for criminal acts that perpetrators carried out on them.

When I didn't take Helen up on her invitation to dinner, Father called and said that he wanted to talk to me. He insisted on speaking to me in person and not on the telephone. He turned down my offer for us to meet in a public place and requested my address instead. Within an hour, he was sitting in my living room with his Bible in his lap.

Father began, "Ever since Kara was in the hospital, Helen and I have been trying to get to the bottom of this mess. The psychiatrist seems to think that her therapy sessions have stirred up a lot of memories from her childhood and that's why she's having the nightmares."

"What's that got to do with me?"

"Well, she doesn't seem to remember much. So we were wondering if you had any memories of being molested."

I didn't want to make the same mistake that I made

with Jack by mentioning the incomplete memory I had with Tom, providing him with a scapegoat. "I've been having nightmares, but that's all."

He pulled a piece of paper from his Bible. "Helen and I put together a list."

"Of what?"

Without looking into my eyes, he answered, "Incidents where you may have been molested." I was shocked as he continued, "You were a baby when Helen and I went on our honeymoon and left you with her grandparents. Her grandfather was an alcoholic who raped Lisa [Helen's aunt] until she was sixteen and ran away. Then when you were in first or second grade—we can't remember exactly when—we got a call from your teacher. She said that she was concerned about you because you didn't play with the other kids. You went off into the woods a lot of times by yourself. She was concerned that you might have been suicidal."

"Did you take me to the doctor?"

"No."

At this point, I found his insolence, to damage my emotional well being in order to take the spotlight off himself, revolting. "You mean you did nothing?"

He shrugged his shoulders and laughed slightly. "You were always a moody child." The feeling like I'd just been kicked in the gut left me speechless, so he continued, "Do you know if anyone else in the family has any memories?"

"Jay told me what happened with him and Helen's stepfather."

"I know," he said. "Helen told me about it the other night, which is also when she told me that he had also molested her and her sister. We didn't know he did that to boys. We only thought that he did that to girls."

"If you knew that, then why was I ever allowed to be alone with him? And why did I spend the night at their house?"

"You were never alone," he said. Helen's mother was always there."

"She was not. I remembering going to his favorite diner and sitting on his lap while she was at work."

"So maybe he molested you, too." I didn't respond, seeing if he would hang himself a second time. "We heard you called Jack, and that he told you about what happened with Tom."

"That's right. He only confirmed my suspicions."

"About what?" he asked.

"A child just doesn't start behaving like that unless someone teaches them. Both Jack and Tom were still children when they started molesting. Studies have proven that it's usually someone close to the family—a relative or parent—who abuses the child. It seems to spread like wildfire into each generation."

Father's face turned red, and he twitched. "Are you accusing Helen and I? The only guilty one is Helen's stepfather."

"I'm not accusing anyone. I only know the statistics. It's been proven that there's a strong correlation between bulimia and sexual abuse. I'm going to do my best to find out who's the engine behind this disgusting train." Suddenly, he took on the same demeanor as he did when he was beating me. The livid volcano was about to erupt. However, I was no longer a helpless child being forced to swallow my own vomit or being kicked like a dog by a barbarian master. This time, I wasn't curling up into a defenseless ball. Though I was prepared to fight back and defend myself if I had to, I restrained from expressing my unresolved anger. "I'm not a child," I stated. "You can't hurt me anymore."

"No one's trying to hurt you. Helen and I are just trying to get to the bottom of this."

"You only came over here to get information out of me. It seems that I'm good enough for Helen to call me whenever someone in the family needs help or money. And I'm good enough to take care of her grandchildren when a crisis arises. Yet I'm the only one who gets excluded from family dinners whenever relatives come down to visit. It's either going to be one way or the other. You can't have it both ways."

"Fine," he said. "I wasn't aware that Helen called you every time there was a crisis. But I'll be sure to tell her not to call anymore."

"So the situation isn't going to change?" *Crush. I could feel his shoe crushing me like an insect under his foot or extinguishing me like I was a used cigarette butt.*

"You older kids have always carried a torch for your dead mother. You never liked Helen."

"She's a sick woman," I said. "And you're in denial."

He got up and showed himself to the door with his bad-news Bible tucked under his arm.

Within days, Father's toxic smoke was beginning to asphyxiate me. The mild asthma that I had previously had under control returned. I continued to have an insatiable hunger for the truth and was seeking artificial resuscitation.

I had heard about Jane, Father's niece and my and Tom's cousin. She was fifteen years older than me and had been suicidal when she was younger. When I telephoned her and explained the recent set of circumstances, she spoke openly about her depression and treatment. Without hesitation, she explained, "I was suicidal and went into therapy because my oldest brother sexually abused my sisters and I from the time I was five years old. He was so evil. It was like living with the Devil himself."

"It looks as though someone got to all the firstborn sons on our father's side. I wonder who it was."

"Daddy whipped us with the belt a lot, but he never did anything like that to us," she said. "I don't know where my brother learned that behavior."

"My father thinks it might have been Helen's step-father."

"Maybe," she said. "But didn't Helen's mother divorce him a few years after your father and Helen got married?"

"I'm not sure. I barely remember him. Anyway, my father said that he didn't know that he was a child molester until recently."

"That's such a lie. He knew about it before he married Helen. That's one of the main reasons why Grandma Riann was against their marriage to begin with, because everyone knew about her stepfather."

"Well, I'm determined to find out where all this started."

"Be careful, Shoshanah," she warned. "This person could still be alive, and they could hurt you." I became sick over the mounting evidence in my criminal investigation, seeing how widespread the disease had become and how many rotten pieces of fruit had fallen from our family tree of deceit. Behind every lead another child's soul had been murdered and an assassin walked free.

I telephoned John, Tom's brother and the cousin I was closest to growing up. I got another piece to the puzzle but no closer to uncovering the truth. John remembered an incident in our childhood when I had complained about Tom trying to take my clothes off. From then on, Tom was ordered to stay away from me. John also admitted that although it happened only once, Tom had gotten to him also. I still wasn't satisfied, so I confronted Tom over the telephone. He didn't deny or admit to any incident with me. He explained that if it did happen, he was a child and had no plan to intentionally hurt me. When he told me that he couldn't remember if or when he was abused himself, I put away my detective badge and halted the investigation.

Kara had already moved away, and she was trying to make a fresh start in another state. Unfortunately, her childhood fiends were on her heels every step of the way. Divorced twice and a struggling single parent again, she caught the eye of a man who was nearly thirty years her senior. He was generous, and she said that she never felt so loved. At first, I welcomed her happiness. Then shortly into their relationship, while she was at work one day he told her youngest daughter to get into bed naked with him. Fortunately, my niece didn't do it and told her older sister what he tried to do. In turn, she told her teacher, whom then contacted the proper authorities. I was concerned that my nieces didn't feel comfortable enough to confide in their mother, but I never questioned Kara's version of the truth. She said that as long as they didn't live together and he went to counseling she and her boyfriend were allowed to continue their relationship.

In the meantime, I was contacted by her social worker. Though I learned that her boyfriend had a previous record as a child offender, I didn't tell the social worker that Kara was still having a relationship with him. I was torn up inside. I knew how much her children had already suffered and how much worse things could get if history repeated itself. I was also angry with her for the position that she was putting me in. For a brief time, I looked the other way. But when I learned they had set a wedding date and were going to get married, I couldn't stay quiet any longer. I contacted the social worker to find out if what Kara had been telling me was the truth. The social worker told me that he wasn't allowed to go anywhere near her children, and if he she married him she would lose custody of them. I didn't regret standing up for my nieces and nephew. But I did have remorse for being quick to judge Kara simply because she wasn't ready to confront her own demons. In my haste to play God, I may have interfered with her children's chance for a better life (possibly in foster care). She was repeating what she learned as a child: to be blind, deaf, and mute to the abuse. When the wedding was called off, Helen didn't waste any time blaming me, informing other family members that I wasn't to be told of Kara's whereabouts.

The next time I heard from Father he was in the first stage of Parkinson's disease. He recently had a professional photograph of himself taken and mailed my siblings and I a copy. When the card he had mailed me got returned to him because he didn't have my latest address, he contacted my sister-in-law to get it. When I received the photo, my initial reaction was passé. But when my sister-in-law called and told me that Father wanted to know if I had received it, Peaches's hopes were revived as she thought that her daddy was finally coming to his senses. In my excitement, I wrote him a short letter, thinking that after all these years he wanted to reconcile. I thanked him for the photo, told him how glad I was to hear from him, expressed my concern over his illness, and gave him my contact numbers and E-mail address.

After a month passed and I hadn't heard from him, I called him. Once he assured me that he had received my letter, he added, "I didn't know how to respond."

"What do you mean?"

"Well, hon, you know the situation," he said. "I'm still a Jehovah's Witness."

"Wait a minute. I'm confused here. My letter didn't say anything about religion. And out of all your children, there's only two who are still Witnesses. I'm aware that you communicate with all of them."

"Yes, I do. But the only one who's in the same situation as you is Beth."

"Exactly," I said.

"Yes, but whenever Beth comes here to help us, we don't discuss religion."

"What about Kate? I asked. "I heard that you found out that she and Beth were baptized as born-again Christians a few years ago."

"I'm not happy that they've been baptized into another faith. And Beth—not Kate—is the only one like you who dedicated her life to Jehovah years ago."

Forced to dedicate my life would have been a more appropriate way of putting it, for if I hadn't he probably would've found another reason to beat me senseless. I could've brought up Kara's name, but I didn't bother. (She got pregnant with her last child before she married. In fact, I knew that was the real reason why she decided to marry someone whom she had known for only a couple of months. If anyone did the math, when her last child was born it was easy to figure out. But Helen brushed it under the carpet, telling everyone that the baby came four weeks early.)

"I'm not looking to have a religious relationship with you," I said instead. "You're the one who always makes an issue out of it—not me."

"Well, I don't know what to tell you. I wish it didn't have to be this way, but you know the rules."

"If nothing's changed, then why did you send me the picture?" I asked.

"Because I'm getting old, sick, and I don't know how much longer I'm going to be around. Even though we have religious differences, you still have my blood running through your veins, and you're still my daughter. I love you, and I would do anything I could for you. I hope you would do the same for me. Wouldn't you?"

Be my doormat again, dear daughter. I love you—kick, I love you—kick. My voice was quivering as he led me to the guillotine. "Likewise," I said sternly. I wanted to confront him about the nightmares that were still haunting me periodically, even though I knew he would never admit anything. Instead, I said, "I need answers. Help me to understand why you only reject me. Otherwise, I'll never be able to have a healthy relationship with any man."

"Look, hon, I'm not rejecting you. You've always thought that Helen and I treat our children differently. We love all of you equally." He couldn't resist the chance to thrust the dagger deep into my heart one last time. "You're the one who told us that you didn't want to hear from us anymore after Kara was in the psychiatrist ward." I heard Helen's voice in the background. I pictured her smiling wickedly, and I could have sworn I heard her shout, "Off with her head!" I felt my nerves shriek as Father dropped the blade of conspiracy, shearing my misguided head of illusions off. I knew that the conversation was going nowhere, and I also knew that I was never going to reach out to him again. I considered hanging up on him, but I didn't want him to think that he had broken my spirit once more. I shifted the subject to the weather. Then after I briefly explained my recent battle with the system. "Life isn't fair, is it?" he replied. I tried not to read too much into the statement. But then he reminded me that I was alone and the only one in our family who remained in Florida. (Everyone else had moved to other states.) At that point, I didn't have a shadow of a doubt that he was intentionally trying to hurt me. He became like a vulture who continued to peck at the carcass he had killed.

"I'm used to it," I said hardheartedly. "I've been alone most of my life." I ended the conversation by asking him to keep in contact.

"If anything happens, someone will call you," he said. In the beginning of our conversation, I had compassion toward him. By the time the conversation was over, I was glad that he had been afflicted with a long-suffering disease.

When I hung up the telephone receiver, I finally realized why I attracted men who were willing only to take and give back nothing but grief to me in return. I had been a magnet for exploiters, particularly men who financially raped me. When I called my sister-in-law to tell her what happened, she reminded me that he was sick, needy, and terrified. And he expects the kids he neglected for so many years to be there for him when he needs them.

Over the next few weeks, Peaches was running scared. Just when I had told her that it was safe to come out and play again, I put her right back in harm's way. She was upset with me for failing to respect her feelings. Though she was hopeful that Father was not going to reject her again, when he did she expected me to stick up for her by telling him to go to hell. I was no better than Father or Helen, telling her to "shush." She misbehaved badly by refusing to eat. She sobbed uncontrollably, allowing me only a few hours of un-interrupted sleep each night. I couldn't let go of the past, so she was going to make sure and sabotage my efforts to have any kind of bright future. In a matter of days, it became extremely difficult to function. My anxiety over the fact that a monster still had control over my life caused me to break out in hives. I spiraled down into a severe depression. As I saw bits and pieces of my life flashing before me again, the suicidal tendencies temporarily resurfaced. Peaches wanted to escape into never-never land, and she was demanding that I go with her. I lacked the courage to go on. But when it came to making my grand exodus, I was a greater coward.

I took out the telephone book and called every church and synagogue in the area until I found help. A rabbi talked me into meeting with him, even though he was on vacation because of the Christmas holidays. Little did I know that he was also a psychiatrist who practiced at a hospital in Miami. We talked for over an hour. He finally convinced me to go to the emergency room. He even held my hand when they tried (but failed because I was dehydrated) to draw my blood, checking for any chemical imbalances and making sure that my thyroid levels were normal. In the three hours that I spent with him (essentially a stranger), I received more compassion and concern than I did in an entire lifetime with Father. Yet after he left and I was alone, I ran out before the second attempt to draw blood. I left the hospital grounds and called for a taxi home. It was nightfall when I got there. I fell fast asleep, relieved to be in my own bed but only to awaken the next morning to the same dreadfulness. My mind was dredging up parts of my childhood that were safely hidden in my subconscious. I vacillated between being a tough cookie who wasn't going to let Father see me crumble and a frightened, lost child. It made no difference that the play had long since left Broadway, for I was still acting like a victim, allowing my worst villain to run the show. Peaches and I were no longer on speaking terms. She had become furious with me because I was still harboring a fugitive. She tried to capture my attention, making me obsess on an image that had been born early in childhood and one that I had long forgotten.

I'm very young (maybe four or five) and in the middle of the ocean. An inflatable tire tube surrounds my small body, keeping me afloat. There's no one else around, except for a man who's tormenting me. I try to kick him away. But he reminds me that if I put up a struggle, he'll leave me all alone to die. When I continue to kick, he shows me that he means business. While he pulls my legs down until my hands lose their grasp and I'm choking on salt water and gasping for air, he taunts, "No one can hear you." As I drown in denial, I have to let him do what he pleases with me. By the time we make it back to shore, the incident is far from my memory bank, lost at sea.

In the past, I went into therapy only whenever the pain became unbearable. Sure enough, as soon as the fire was under control and I had processed what was going on currently, I stopped going. Likewise, I stopped taking the antidepressants, which had been prescribed to me a half dozen times, without giving them a chance to work. I was superwoman. I didn't need crutches to support me through my self-loathing stages. As an alternative, I became a couch potato and self-help junkie, watching talk shows that dealt with my issues and gobbling up as many books and tapes that I could stomach.

This time, however, I didn't have the strength to fight back. And having seen how toxic the lives of some of my relatives had become, I knew how powerful the menacing monster could be. I wasn't willing to risk my life and slay this dragon without a potent elixir. This time required me to recruit all of my healing resources.

I went searching through my collection of Anthony Robbins's tapes and books. (Shortly after my trip to Maui, I was privileged enough to attend one of his seminars. At that time, the positive reinforcement didn't have lasting effects, probably since I was not yet aware that I had a hypothyroid condition.) So at this point, a couple of years later, I was ready to relearn his techniques and actually apply them this time. Meanwhile, I was prescribed an antidepressant that didn't exacerbate my vertigo or send me into the twilight zone. *And I stayed on it.* After I was diagnosed with post traumatic stress disorder, an acquaintance had told me about the remarkable results she was having with EMDR (eye movement desensitization reprocessing) therapy. I was fortunate to find a therapist on my insurance plan who specialized in it. Additionally, I collected the cassette tapes of readings that I had over the past few years with renowned psychics like Sylvia Browne and others. Of course, when one psychic told me of the rewards that were in store for me if I didn't give up, I didn't believe it because of all the bad experiences I had encountered. So my doubt sent me to get other opinions. For awhile, I was growing dependent on them to keep me going, failing to realize that what I was lacking was the belief in myself. I kept their booster shots of encouragement within arm's reach. Finally, out of mere coincidence, a group of Tibetan monks were visiting a healing facility in Miami. I immediately scheduled a healing session. After a few exercises, the monk wrote down several chants for me to practice daily. These were intended to invite healing, prosperity, and peace.

With my weapons in place, I stepped into the lion's den. It didn't take long for the beast to reemerge. The first nightmare I had went like this: I'm laying in the woods with poisonous snakes. A faceless man warns me that if I don't lay completely still, I'll die because the snakes will bite me. So while a cobra wriggles its way over my body, I lay there frozen with fear. As the snake slithers away, along comes a black widow. I woke up before the spider had a chance to bite me. My previous criminal investigation had indicated that I might have been sexually violated in some way, at least once, by my cousin and/or Helen's stepfather. Since I thought I had come to terms with this revelation, I didn't understand what message my soul was trying to send me and why I couldn't let this issue go.

A couple of weeks later, I had a similar nightmare: I'm a child again on a camping trip with my family. It's nightfall, and while the rest of my siblings lay in their unconscious state, I wake up and find two diamond-back rattlesnakes coiled side by side on the wall next to our beds. I try to wake up the others, but the only one who hears my screams is Jay. After that, I woke up. What was significant to me about this nightmare was that Father and Helen weren't in the camper with us, that is, *in human form*.

The next nightmare I had was much more revealing: I'm a child in bed with Father. I look down at the exaggerated size of his penis and realize that he's going to put it inside me. "That's going to hurt," I say. An adult version of me stands at the edge of the bed and speaks to the child version of me. "You won't feel anything . . . I promise." While Father is doing his dirty deed and filling me with his filthy seeds, the child version of me says, "You're right. How come I can't feel anything?" The adult version of me answers, "Because I protected you and took you to another place outside of yourself." I awoke in a peaceful state.

While a couple of regressive hypnosis sessions, which I had shortly after Kara was admitted to the psychiatric ward, caused childhood memories to surface, I found the technique too unpleasant to continue. Before I made anymore allegations and felt comfortable writing about it, my conscience was circumspect. And I knew that it would be impossible to produce anything positive as long as I was still writing with a poisonous pen.

As a rose on the bloom, I was trying to make up for the years I lost following my divorce. My pearls of wisdom helped me make healthier choices, and my tastes had become more discriminating. I was dating a man, and although the relationship was more physical than anything else, it was what I needed at the time to completely heal. During a painful thrusting period of sexual intercourse, I saw Father's face and not my lover's. I excused myself and went into the bathroom, feeling as though I needed to vomit and flush Father down the toilet. I started shaking, and tears followed. Peaches was summoning me to avenge her killer. I had to calm her down and assure her that she could trust me and that it wasn't Father out there waiting for us. She and I mutually agreed that it was finally time to let Daddy go.   When I came out of the bathroom, I was tempted to dismiss my lover and fought off the urge to push him away. Though he asked if I was okay, I didn't discuss what I had just experienced. I continued with our playful session, determined to live in the moment and give myself permission to experience joy.

I later learned that an identical physical sensation, scent, or sound (which was there during the actual event) could encourage flashbacks. This, and the other flashback I had during hypnosis, wasn't enough to convict Father unless other victims were willing to step forward. Besides, I had already lost too many years to the reprobate. The circumstantial evidence I had been gathering gave my soul the closure that it was seeking. The poison that had been ejaculated into my psyche, leaving me unconscious for the better part of my life, lost its potency.

After my subconscious lifted the veil of denial, it was like a curtain went up. I was able to see things with clarity, looking at every area in my life with an objectivity that I didn't have before. I was more focused, less distracted, and able to live in the moment with ease. I also enjoyed sex more without feeling guilty or dirty about it.

It didn't take long for the universe to present me with a situation that would test my newfound strength. Shortly after I had slain my last dragon, Beth contacted me through an E-mail. She sent a letter to my siblings and I, soliciting financial support for Father and Helen. She attached a personal memo to mine, apologizing for any discomfort the letter might bring me, for she had heard about my conversation with Father. Peaches refused to rest quietly, afraid that this time would be like all the others. (I wasn't going to follow through on my promises, and she was going to be let down again.) I responded politely, explaining that I was no longer going to give Father the power to hurt me anymore, and I no longer traveled down one-way streets. Though it was Beth I told those words to and not Father, Peaches started to trust me because I finally stood up for her. The E-mail did upset me for a couple of days, but I wasn't immobilized and so grief-stricken to even entertain the idea of bailing out. I stopped taking one step forward and two steps back. As I realized that his rejection and abuse was having less of an impact on me, my resiliency was a testimony that I had made progress.

The year that followed has been the best year, thus far, of my life. I sold my condo and made a healthy profit. Then I went on my first European vacation. After I completed more writing courses and was se-duced by the seascape from my high-rise apartment, I became inspired to tell my story. In doing so, I have concluded that the greatest facilitator of faith is one who has lived by facts instead of one who has been created by fiction.

My childhood left me disfigured by physical, sexual, emotional, and religious abuse, setting me up for a lifetime of struggle. Yet it also provided me with experiences that caused me to develop characteristics I'm certain I wouldn't have cultivated otherwise. Once I no longer considered myself a bag of damaged goods, and I realized that I was the one with the power, I was able to denounce my birthright of oppression. I hold the power to my thoughts, words, and actions—and with these the choice to accept and change.

Now whenever I walk the seashore, there is only one set of footprints in the sand. Peaches is finally getting to discover a promised-land playground that she never could have imagined existed. United, we are experiencing a second childhood, *only this time it's on our terms.*

Author Update: I hope my story will help women realize that whether we are brought up to be adored or abused we all have a prince-charming fantasy. Regardless of our background, abusers come from all walks of life. We have no control over the family we're born into. But as adults we do have the power to walk away from anyone who makes us feel powerless. I've paid a heavy price and lost several years because I ignored my intuition. Once I understood how powerful it is, miracles began to happen in my life.

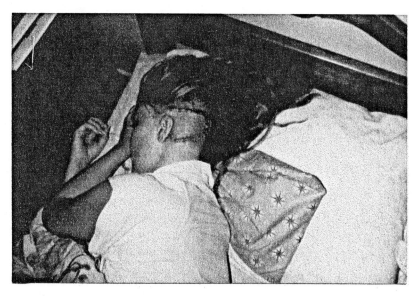

October, 1992; two weeks after vestibular nerve section surgery

December, 1989; Arthur (in the jacket) and I with his associate
at the anuual awards banquet honoring Civil Air Patrol members

April, 1965; Father with Rachel, Jay, Julia,
Joshua, and me one week after Mom died

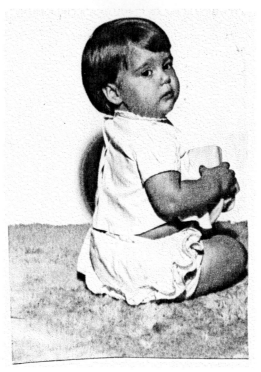

February, 1966; I am thirteen months old here

0-595-30166-5